Were They Wise Men
or Kings?

Were They Wise Men or Kings?

The Book of Christmas Questions

JOSEPH J. WALSH

Westminster John Knox Press
LOUISVILLE
LONDON · LEIDEN

Scripture quotations, unless otherwise indicated, are from the New Revised Standard Version of the Bible, copyright © 1989 by the Division of Christian Education of the National Council of the Churches of Christ in the U.S.A., and used by permission.

Book design by Sharon Adams
Cover design by Kathy York
Illustrations: Bob Pepper

First edition
Published by Westminster John Knox Press
Louisville, Kentucky

This book is printed on acid-free paper that meets the American National Standards Institute Z39.48 standard. ∞

PRINTED IN THE UNITED STATES OF AMERICA

01 02 03 04 05 06 07 08 09 10 — 10 9 8 7 6 5 4 3 2 1

Library of Congress Cataloging-in-Publication Data

Walsh, Joseph J.
  Were they wise men or kings? : the book of Christmas questions / Joseph J. Walsh.
    p. cm.
  Includes bibliographical references.
  ISBN 0-664-22312-5 (alk. paper)
  1. Christmas. 2. Questions and answers. I. Title.

GT4985 . W35 2001
394.2663—dc21

2001022245

*To my mother,
and in loving memory
of my father,
who have known how
to keep Christmas well,
if any ever possessed
the knowledge*

Contents

————— • ◆ • —————

❄ Peace on Earth

Acknowledgments

———◆·———

Many have contributed to this book. Angela Christman, Tom Pegram, and Bryan Crockett of Loyola College, ever the most generous and learned of colleagues, read portions of the manuscript, improved it, and saved me from embarrassment at more than one point. I wish I could blame them for the errors that remain but, alas, I cannot. Drew Leder provided other kinds of support and advice. Noelle Chandler was a marvelous research assistant, and I would also like to thank Loyola College's Center for the Humanities for enabling Noelle to work with me. Cindy McCabe, Ginnie Harper, and Peggy Feild of the Loyola/Notre Dame Library Interlibrary Loan Office were Herculean in their efforts to find countless books and articles, many obscure and out of print. I would like to express particular gratitude to my editor, Stephanie Egnotovich, whose encouragement, dedication, kindness, and advice have been indispensable to the completion of this book. She has also done wonders with my often awkward and unclear prose, though she can't be blamed for the infelicities that slipped through. I can only hope that I am half so useful to my students in correcting their writing. Most of all, though, my wife and colleague, Gayla McGlamery, has made this book possible. She has read every page, improved every word, and showed the loving patience and wisdom that make life worth living. Since she's my spouse, I reserve the right to blame her for everything that's wrong with this book, even though she doesn't deserve it. Thanks also to my seven-year-old son, Joseph, who has provided his own delightful kind of inspiration and support.

Introduction

*C*hristmas is about everything.

I realized this fact only a couple of years ago when I started teaching a course on Christmas to freshmen at Loyola College in Maryland. I thought students would be attracted to the topic, and I felt I had a head start on the material because of my experience teaching classics and history and because of some research I had done on the history of the early Christians. I was in for a surprise. What I hadn't fully realized is that Christmas touches upon virtually every aspect of human history, belief, thought, and behavior. In my research for the course, I found myself in awful World War I trenches, in the mysterious forests of prehistoric Europe, on the American frontier, in splendid Spanish cathedrals, in astronomical observatories, in the minds of marketers, and, of course, in Bethlehem. And it was all fascinating.

Sometimes we are apprehensive that if we learn too much about something, we will no longer be able to enjoy it. Movies can cast enchanting spells with their illusions, but we may wonder: If I understand how the director makes the magic happen, will the delightful spell be broken? Those of us who love Christmas might feel the same apprehension. If I understand too much about the origin, evolution, and traditions of the holiday, if I am aware of the sometimes strange paths by which many Christmas customs have come to the season, will my joy be muted?

I can make no guarantees, but I have found that knowing more about the myths, traditions, and history of the holiday season has made my Christmases more meaningful—and much more fun to boot. Besides, when we are confronted by the awkward situation that mistletoe presents and someone asks, "Where did this custom come from, anyway?" someone needs to have the answer.

There's no right way to read this book. You can start anywhere and read the questions in any order. Each question was written to stand on its own, but many of them also raise additional questions that are answered in other sections. Each of the questions about Santa, for example, makes sense on its own, but all the Santa questions together give you a fuller portrait of this large figure.

I don't answer every interesting or significant question that you can think of about Christmas. I've got hundreds more myself. As I've already suggested, Christmas is about everything. I hope, however, that I've answered many of the most frequently asked questions while answering others that, though perhaps less frequently asked, explain just as much about our most important and cherished holiday.

1. Who was the original St. Nick?

St. Nicholas was a fourth-century bishop and miracle worker. The surviving stories of his activities and accomplishments are so marvelous and even, at times, bizarre that their authenticity is doubtful. And yet there is little doubt that these stories have helped shape the Santa we know—and that they are great stories.

Some of them actually help explain how St. Nicholas, and thus Santa Claus, became the patron of children and gift-giving. One story involves a man and his three young daughters. The man had fallen on hard times and could barely afford to feed and shelter the girls. Worst of all, he knew he could never afford to provide them with dowries, and without dowries, he feared, no one would marry them. He would be forced to sell them into prostitution.

St. Nicholas heard of the daughters' pitiful situation and resolved to help them avoid such a terrible fate. But how, he wondered, could he do that without humiliating the man and drawing unwanted attention to himself? He resolved this dilemma by acting under the cover of darkness. He went to the family's house in the middle of the night and tossed through the window a bag of gold, enough to provide the first daughter with a dowry. One saved! Soon afterwards, on *another* night, St. Nicholas tossed a second bag of gold through the window, saving the middle daughter from degradation.

The father naturally became increasingly curious about the identity of his benefactor. He began spending his nights hiding near the window, waiting for his daughters' savior to return. When Nicholas came by with the third bag, for the youngest daughter, the father leapt out from hiding and caught him. At the bishop's insistence, the grateful man promised not to disclose his identity, but despite his gratitude and his promise, he let others know about Nicholas' generosity. As far as we can tell, this story first appeared centuries after St. Nicholas' death, but its popularity forever bound the bishop to children and generosity, and so to Christmas.

A second story about St. Nicholas' kind patronage of children is quite macabre. At a time when food was scarce, an innkeeper was keeping his customers fed by kidnapping and murdering children and salting their corpses to serve as pork in a variety of dishes. No one realized that the innkeeper was making cannibals of them all until St. Nicholas visited the inn one evening for dinner. As soon as he saw the food, he recognized it for what it really was. He immediately searched the premises and found the tub where the innkeeper salted the dead children. In the tub he discovered the corpses of three little boys! Nicholas made the sign of the cross over the tub, and the boys came back to life. The innkeeper, according to the custom of the time, was stoned to death.

You may have heard St. Nicholas referred to as "St. Nicholas of Bari," a city in southern Italy. This is the same St. Nicholas, although he did not acquire the designation "of Bari" until more than six hundred years after his death. St. Nicholas actually lived in Myra, an ancient town located in southwestern Turkey near the city of Demre. But in 1087, sailors from Bari stole what were reputed to be the saint's bones from his crypt in Turkey and brought them back to their hometown. To house the plundered remains of the saint, the people of Bari erected a church to St. Nicholas. The church still stands, and to this day Bari's principal festival on May 8 is a reenactment of the transfer of Nicholas' remains.

But wait! The Venetians claimed that *they* had the real bones of the saint in the church of St. Nicholas on the Lido near Venice. The desire of both Bari and Venice to have Nicholas' remains might suggest to us today that both cities had a particular fondness for children. But it was the fact that St. Nicholas was prized as the patron saint of sailors and merchants that made his remains so desirable to these medieval port cities. You see, according to another story, a young Nicholas was traveling to Jerusalem by sea when a terrible storm descended on the ship. The sailors and other travelers knew they were doomed, but Nicholas calmed the storm through his prayers and so saved their lives. The traders and sailors of Venice and Bari believed that his bones would protect them, too, from catastrophe at sea.

One might think that Santa Claus has completely eclipsed the original St. Nicholas, but that is not entirely so. St. Nicholas is the patron saint of several nations, including Russia, and to this day children in parts of Belgium, the Netherlands, and Germany receive their holiday gifts on December 6, the saint's feast day. And every year on December 4–6 the city of Demre holds a Santa Claus symposium, where scholars, church folk, and Nicholas enthusiasts discuss his life, works, and legacy. And if your name is Nicholas, you've got the saint, not Santa, to thank. As does Santa Claus himself, since his name is in fact an anglicized form of *Sinter Klaas,* a Dutch version of St. Nicholas.

2. Why does Santa Claus wear that peculiar outfit?

Santa Claus has never had the opportunity to dress himself. We have always clothed him in outfits that reflect our sense of who he is—and who we are. The red and white Santa suit he dons in every town in America these days is actually, for the most part, the attire that nineteenth-century writers and illustrators imagined for him. The poor man has not had the opportunity to change his clothes since.

In the Middle Ages, before St. Nicholas evolved into Santa, artists usually depicted him in the stately garb of a medieval bishop: as a tall, thin, bearded cleric with a miter on his head and a staff in his hands. He looked a little different from most bishops, though, for he often carried three golden balls, which symbolized the three dowries he gave to save a poor man's daughters from prostitution. The balls acted as a kind of identity code, telling pious viewers, who were often illiterate, that they were looking at a picture of St. Nicholas as opposed to, say, St. Augustine, who also would have been depicted as a stately bishop. This older, proper St. Nicholas, although overwhelmed by our chubby red and white Santa, has not disappeared from our culture completely. At Christmastime, a number of shops still sell cards, pictures, and statues of the clerical St. Nicholas.

So how did this nearly gaunt, dignified bishop come to have a portly body and be dressed in bright red and white? Like many immigrants to our country, St. Nicholas/Santa Claus entered through the port of New York, or, as it was then called, New Amsterdam. The Dutch business folk who settled Manhattan island and the Hudson River Valley brought with them their own customs and legends and brought their St. Nicholas as well. Some historians, noting the dearth of references to Santa in surviving documents from Dutch New York, suggest that St. Nicholas may have played a negligible role in the lives and imaginations of early Dutch New Yorkers. Perhaps. We nonetheless owe a debt to the Dutch since it was they who brought the *idea* of Santa

Claus to New York, an idea that inspired a handful of early New Yorkers to transform the Dutch saint and gift-giver into an American symbol and icon. These New Yorkers also transformed the way the saint looked.

Here's how.

Step one. In his 1809 *Knickerbocker's History of New York,* Washington Irving claims (fictitiously!) that a Dutch ship entered New York Harbor with a figurehead of St. Nicholas wearing "a low, broadbrimmed hat, a huge pair of Flemish trunk hose, and a pipe that reached to the end of the bowsprit." At this point, Santa looks like a large, smoking Dutchman.

Step two. In 1821, a poem titled "The Children's Friend" is published with an engraving of a solid-looking Santa with a thick coat, tall fur hat, and copious beard. By now Santa is furry, bundled, and bearded.

Step three. In 1823, the *Troy Sentinel,* an upstate New York newspaper, published "A Visit from St. Nicholas" (also known as "'Twas the Night before Christmas"), which tells of a short, old, very fat, spritely "jolly old elf." "His eyes—how they twinkled! His dimples how merry! His cheeks were like roses, his nose like a cherry!" He wore fur everywhere, a fine complement to his snow-white beard, and held a pipe in his mouth. Now we have a fuzzy, rotund, cheery old elf. Elf, indeed, since not only does he no longer seem to be Dutch, he doesn't even seem to be human!

Step four. Thomas Nast, America's foremost magazine illustrator of the nineteenth century—not only did he help drive the infamously corrupt "Boss" Tweed from Tammany Hall, but he also invented the donkey and elephant symbols of the Republican and Democratic parties—completes the picture. Nast drew numerous illustrations of Santa Claus, generally depicting him as a plump, merry old man with a beard. Nast's Santa usually wore buckled shoes, a red suit, a fur-lined stocking cap, and a wide belt joined by a huge buckle. (Sound familiar?) Although some of Nast's earlier illustrations present a Santa small enough to slide down a chimney—that elf again?—his later Santa is full-sized.

So compelling have been the words of "A Visit from St. Nicholas" and Nast's illustrations that subsequent Santas have undergone only the most minor of alterations.

3. Where did Rudolph the Red-Nosed Reindeer come from?

A promotional gimmick.

In 1939, Montgomery Ward & Company assigned Robert L. May, who worked in its advertising department, the job of writing a Christmas animal story. The company planned to distribute the story to its customers' children, not primarily to delight them but to increase sales. A marketing effort.

Inspired by the story of the ugly duckling (and, according to a 1951 interview, by his own childhood frustrations), May decided his story would be about a young, outcast animal triumphing over adversity—Rudolph. He wanted to connect the story to the myth of Santa Claus, and a reindeer seemed a natural choice. But what kind of adversity? What trait could cause the other reindeer to shun him? May pondered the fact that Santa delivers his gifts at night and considered giving Rudolph large, bright eyes like headlights that could see in the dark, but decided that an oversized, red nose would seem a more credible source of mockery. So Rudolph got his nose.

The story was an immense hit. Montgomery Ward gave away over 2,400,000 copies in 1939 and about 3,500,000 when the company reissued it in 1947. In 1949 Johnny Marks composed the famous song "Rudolph the Red-Nosed Reindeer," which was recorded by, among others, the singing cowboy, Gene Autry (who had co-written and recorded both the famous "Here Comes Santa Claus" and the unsuccessful "Nestor, the Long-Eared Christmas Donkey.") The immense popularity of the song and a later television version of the story firmly fixed Rudolph alongside Santa in the imaginations of American children.

May clearly intended his story to be a source of inspiration to children whose special virtues other children failed to recognize. Like Rudolph, May seems to suggest that you too will one day be appreciated. Not all children may find it comforting, though, that it is only through exceptional success that Rudolph silences the jeers.

4. Who wrote "A Visit from St. Nicholas"?

*W*e don't know for certain, although we long thought we did.

In 1823, the *Troy Sentinel* published the poem anonymously. Indeed, the editor claimed not to know who wrote the poem, which the paper introduced as follows: "We know not to whom we are indebted for the following description of that unwearied patron of children—that homey and delightful personage of parental kindness—Santa Claus, his costume and his equipage, as he goes about visiting the firesides of this happy land, laden with Christmas bounties; but from whomsoever it may have come, we give thanks for it."

Virtually every edition of "A Visit from St. Nicholas" cites Clement Clarke Moore as the author of the poem.

Moore was a respected member of two important New York families and himself played significant roles in the history of New York City and of the Episcopalian Church. His father, the Reverend Benjamin Moore, had been the Episcopal Bishop of New York City and had served as president of Columbia College, today's Columbia University. From his father, Clement Moore inherited a dedication to teaching in service of his faith. He became a serious scholar of Greek, Latin, and Hebrew, and even wrote the first American dictionary of Hebrew, *The Compendious Lexicon of the Hebrew Language*, in 1809. He spent his professional life teaching ancient languages and Asian literature at New York's General Theological Seminary.

From his mother, Moore inherited a considerable Manhattan estate. At the beginning of the nineteenth century—he was born in 1779—only the southern tip of Manhattan was urban. As difficult as it is for us to imagine today, most of the island was undeveloped, even hilly country. Captain Thomas Clarke, the poet's maternal grandfather, had purchased an impressive section on it and built an estate that he named Chelsea. Eventually, that estate came to Clement Moore. Moore loved the property, but he recognized that in New York's rapid growth northward, urbanization would gobble up his country estate—and that profit could be made from progress. Rather than fight a hopeless war to preserve his land, Moore helped determine how the land would be integrated into the exploding metropolis. Today we would call him a developer. The modern west-side neighborhood known as Chelsea today marks the site of his childhood home and keeps its name alive.

On Christmas Eve of 1822, according to Clement Moore and Moore family tradition, he went out to purchase a turkey for the family Christmas feast. It was a cold, snowy day, and so he took his sleigh. During the sleigh ride to and from the market, he composed the verses in his head, a feat so impressive that some modern skeptics have doubted the authenticity of the story. When he returned home, he jotted down the words, and before his children went off to bed that evening, he recited the poem to their great delight. This spontaneous composition was intended as a Christmas gift only for his children, not for the world. But a friend of the family, Harriet Butler of Troy, New York, apparently got hold of the poem, and somehow it appeared the very next year in the December 23, 1823, edition of the *Troy Sentinel.* Moore did not acknowledge his authorship until 1837.

But while virtually all the world has accepted Clement Clarke Moore as the author of "Visit," the family of Henry Livingston, Jr. has been claiming for generations that he is the true author.

Henry Livingston was an interesting personality as well. He was born in Poughkeepsie, New York, in 1748, and had a large family and many careers: Revolutionary War patriot, lumber man, farmer, illustrator, poet, even a Commissioner of Bankruptcy Court. He wrote quite a few whimsical and humorous verses, many of them for children.

According to Livingston family tradition, on Christmas day of 1807 or 1808 Henry Livingston came down to breakfast with his family and a guest. He announced at the table that he had composed a Christmas poem for them and then read "A Visit from St. Nicholas" over breakfast. The guest was so delighted with the poem that she asked him for a copy of it. He consented, and then she, presumably, brought the poem to the attention of the outside world.

So who wrote "A Visit from St. Nicholas"?

In a recent book titled *Author Unknown,* Don Foster forcefully restates and strengthens the Livingston claim. Foster, a professor of English literature at Vassar College, specializes in identifying the authors of anonymous writings by analyzing those writings' grammar, word selection, spelling, and style. Just as each of us has a unique fingerprint, each person writes and speaks in distinctive ways that enable the trained analyst to identify even authors who attempt to conceal their identities. Professor Foster has applied his method of linguistic analysis to writers as diverse as William Shakespeare and the Unabomber.

He makes a number of points as he argues for Livingston and against Moore. He notes, for instance, that

- Clement Moore was a grim disciplinarian who could barely tolerate the presence of children; Livingston was a warm, jolly father. Which sort of man, he asks, would have been more likely to compose "Visit"?
- Livingston was of three-fourth Dutch descent and was thus more likely to have honored St. Nicholas, a saint particularly cherished in Holland; the first publication of the poem in the *Troy Sentinel*, moreover, has two of the reindeers' names spelled according to Dutch practice, "D*u*nder and Bli*xem*"; whereas Moore, when late in life he wrote the poem out in his own hand while claiming authorship, wrote, "D*o*nder and Bli*tzen*," essentially German versions of the Dutch names. This shows that Moore did not really know the names of the reindeer he supposedly invented and so substituted German, which he knew, for Dutch, which he did not know.
- The words, phrases, and rhythm of "Visit" closely parallel those found in Livingston's other poetry, but are utterly alien to Moore's.

Take a look at Foster's engaging book to read the other arguments he makes in support of Livingston.

So is the case closed? Foster thinks so, and his book is very persuasive. As of this writing, however, Moore's advocates have not yet had time to respond. It's a good bet that they will.

5. Why does Santa travel by sleigh and reindeer?

he notion of Santa in a sleigh pulled by reindeer came either from an American poem or from Finnish legend. Or from both! Today, Santa is universally considered to get around by sleigh and reindeer because of the immense influence of "A Visit from St. Nicholas." No American poem is better known and loved nor more a part of American popular culture and consciousness. Love it or hate it, we can't escape it. Or the fact that this quintessential Santa uses sleigh and reindeer:

> "When, what to my wondering eyes should appear
> But a miniature sleigh, and eight tiny reindeer."

If Henry Livingston Jr. wrote "Visit" in 1807 or 1808, then it was he who came up with the idea of having reindeer pull Santa's sleigh.

But if Clement Clarke Moore wrote "A Visit from St. Nicholas" in 1822, then the author of another anonymous poem had the original idea. In 1821, this poem was published in New York in an illustrated book, *A New-Year's Present to the Little Ones from Five to Twelve*. The following lines of the poem were accompanied by an engraving of Santa in a sleigh pulled by *one* reindeer:

> Old Santeclaus with much delight
> His reindeer drives this Frosty night.
> O'er chimney tops, and tracks of snow,
> To bring his yearly gifts.

But where did either Livingston or the anonymous author of "Old Santeclaus" come up with this fancy?

It is certainly possible that it was the product of the poetic imagination. Considering that Christmas is a winter holiday, it's easy to imagine substituting a sleigh for a wagon (which Santa drove in other versions) and reindeer for horses, since polar bears and penguins are unsuited to pull a sleigh. It is just as likely, though, that the authors of "Visit" and "A New Year's Present" knew of and were adapting an ancient Finnish legend. In Lapp mythology, every year winter snow was brought down from the mountains by "Old Man Winter" as he drove his reindeer to lower ground. The Finnish "Old Man Winter" was not Santa Claus, but one can see how the Lapp story could suggest that Santa should have reindeer as well.

6. Is Santa Claus the true founder of New York City?

ccording to Washington Irving, yes!
We know Washington Irving chiefly from his two classic short stories, "Rip Van Winkle" and "The Legend of Sleepy Hollow." His first book, though, was published in 1809 with the remarkable title, "A History of New York, From the Beginning of the World to the end of the Dutch Dynasty. Containing Among many Surprising and Curious Matters, the unutterable Ponderings of Walter the Doubter, the Disastrous Projects of William the Testy, and the Chivalric Achievements of Peter the Headstrong, the three Dutch governors of New Amsterdam; being the only Authentic History of the Times that ever hath been, or ever will be Published. By Diedrich Knickerbocker." The second, expanded edition of *A History of New York* came out in 1812, and this is the book that claims St. Nicholas told the Dutch where to found New Amsterdam, that is, New York.

According to Irving's imaginative chronicle, a Dutch expedition led by Oloffe van Kortlandt became stranded on the tip of what today is lower Manhattan. At that time, of course, the island was largely wilderness and had no European inhabitants. To fortify himself to lead his charges to safety, van Kortlandt "deemed it incumbent on him to eat profoundly for the public good." And so, he devoured too many oysters and washed them down "with a fervant potation." Oloffe, quite naturally, fell asleep. He then had a dream. Irving describes it as follows:

> And lo, the good St. Nicholas came riding over the tops of trees, in that self-same wagon wherein he brings his yearly presents to children, and he descended hard by . . . And he lit his pipe by the fire, and sat himself down and smoked; and as he smoked, the smoke from his pipe ascended into the air and spread like a cloud overhead. And Oloffe bethought him, and he hastened and climbed up to the top of one of the tallest trees, and saw that the smoke spread over a great

extent of country; and as he considered it more attentively, he fancied that the great volume of smoke assumed a variety of marvellous forms, where in dim obscurity he saw shadowed out palaces and domes and lofty spires, all of which lasted but a moment, and then faded away, until the whole rolled off, and nothing but the green woods were left. And when St. Nicholas had smoked his pipe, he twisted it in his hatband, and laying his finger beside his nose, gave the astonished Van Kortlandt a very significant look; then, mounting his wagon, he returned over the tree-tops and disappeared.

When he awoke, Oloffe told his mates about the dream and explained that it meant that St. Nicholas was instructing them to build their city there. The smoke of the pipe indicated "how vast would be the extent of the city, inasmuch as the volumes of its smoke would spread over a wide extent of country." And so New York was born.

Although Irving slyly dedicated the book to the New York Historical Society, there was very little history in it. In fact, Irving simply made up most of his satirical "history" of Dutch New York. Even the author, Diedrich Knickerbocker, was the product of Irving's imagination. Although St. Nicholas can count many benefactions to his name, New York City is not among them.

But how did Washington Irving cook up this very strange yarn? And why in the world would he attribute the founding of New York City to St. Nicholas, of all people?

First, as the patron saint of the Dutch, St. Nicholas is invoked again and again in this account of Dutch New York. In the 1812 edition of *The History of New York,* moreover, Irving inserted new, almost nostalgic material about the charm and warmth of Christmas in old New Amsterdam. Why not expand the myth of St. Nicholas and allow him to found the city?

There is another element to all of this, as well. In ancient epics it was common for heroes to receive instructions and inspiration from the gods. Ancient Greek settlers always expected the gods to provide some sign of approval of the sites they selected to found new cities. Irving's *History* is full of parody of these ancient epics. And so Oloffe receives "divine" inspiration, just like ancient Rome's national mythical hero Aeneas—except, of course, that you won't find Aeneas overwhelmed by oysters and drink.

7. Who wrote Santa's biography?

L Frank Baum, the creator of Dorothy, Toto, and the Wizard of Oz.

Baum titled his biography of Santa *The Life and Adventures of Santa Claus* and published it in 1902, a couple of years after he had created a sensation with the publication of *The Wonderful Wizard of Oz.*

In *Life and Adventures* Baum describes Santa Claus' origin, but his tale has nothing to do with the historical St. Nicholas. Rather, in the wake of his popular success in creating Oz, Baum made up an entirely new history and world for Santa, quite different from any earlier account.

Baum's Santa started life as an abandoned baby who was rescued by a nymph named Necile. With the permission of the Master Woodsman, one of three rulers of the universe Baum created, Necile raised Santa in the beautiful and peaceful Forest of Burzee.

In Baum's story, the name Santa has nothing to do with St. Nicholas. Necile actually named the baby "Claus," which apparently meant "a little one" in the language of the nymphs. (In a footnote to the story, Baum considerately explains how we misnamed him Nicholas. It seems that his full name was actually "Neclaus," which means "Necile's little one." We humans got confused because Neclaus and Nicholas sound somewhat similar and, unfortunately, none of us have had the opportunity to learn the Nymph language.)

Baum's Santa not only came to deliver toys—he invented them! The very first toy was, in fact, a wooden cat that Santa carved. When he discovered how much pleasure children took in toys, he started making more and more, and, well, the rest is history.

It was Santa's reindeer who first suggested that he enter children's homes by chimney to deliver his toys. And the reindeers' real names, according to Baum, were Glossie, Flossie, Racer, Pacer, Reckless, Speckless, Fearless, Peerless, Ready, and Steady.

According to Baum, folks are mistaken in thinking that Santa lives at the North Pole. In fact, he lives in the Laughing Valley of Hohaho, where it does snow, but not all the time.

Baum's Santa also faced dangers. The Awgwas, an awful race of invisible ogres who delighted in inspiring children to make mischief, tried to murder Santa. They were angry because his toys made the children invulnerable to their influence, "for children possessing such lovely playthings as he gave them had no wish to obey the evil thoughts the Awgwas tried to thrust into their minds." (Baum *did* have children—*Life and Adventures* is even dedicated to his son Harry Neal.) To save Santa, several races of benevolent immortals—Nymphs, Knooks, Ryls, and Fairies—made war on and destroyed the Awgwas.

In Baum's account, not only does Santa have nothing to do with St. Nicholas, but Christmas seems to have nothing to do with the Nativity. And yet, although the book can be viewed as contributing to the secularization and materialization of a religious holiday, it gives us much to think about. Amidst the fantasy and whimsy are many reminders of the fact that adult life can be grim and burdensome and that children, Santa's special clients, are often the innocent victims of poverty. Baum was apprehensive about the values and direction of America as it entered the twentieth century. (In his 1911 book, *Sea Fairies*, Baum tells of an octopus insulted at being compared to Standard Oil!) His response in *Life and Adventures* was to make an eloquent plea for the heroism of kindness and service to community.

Life and Adventures offered new and fanciful explanations for the origins of many other elements of Santa's life and significance, but it did so by weaving them together in a charming narrative. We are fortunate to be able to read this oft-forgotten story again, since Gramercy Books republished the text with illustrations in 1999.

8. Why does Santa come down the chimney?

The simplest and, indeed, the only certain answer is because he can get in that way.

People have been puzzling over this question for quite some time. The influence of "A Visit from St. Nicholas" may have made Santa's entrance by chimney part of America's standard Christmas lore, but Santa's connection with chimneys actually dates back several centuries before the poem.

We can see the association already in a charming seventeenth-century Dutch painting by Jan Steen titled "The Feast of St. Nicholas." It depicts St. Nicholas' Day (the giving of Christmas gifts still takes place in several countries on December 6): A little girl is delighted with her gifts, while her brother bewails the fact that he has received nothing. Most interesting for our question, though, in the background an adult and two toddlers are looking up the chimney, amazement on their faces. It is clear that St. Nicholas—or at the very least the gifts he brought—came down the chimney. (You can view the painting in the Rijksmuseum in Amsterdam.)

The chimney motif may have originated with the early story about St. Nicholas tossing bags of gold through a poor man's window to prevent him from having to sell his daughters into prostitution. It is not so great a leap to have him toss the money down through the chimney instead, especially since in northern climes people probably would have shut and barred their windows in the cold of December. And, in fact, a later version of the story has St. Nicholas using the chimney in precisely this way when he found the windows locked on his third visit. Besides, as early as the seventh century, stories give the saint the ability to teleport himself any distance instantly, the kind of magic many a parent has offered as an explanation of how a portly man with a huge bag of presents gets down and up narrow chimneys.

Some scholars have looked to pre-Christian pagan lore and practice to find the origins of Santa's chimney entrance. Hearths, for example, were thought to house spirits or gods who were critical to the prosperity of the household, and fire itself was held sacred. It would not be surprising, then, for a myth to develop in which bounty is bestowed by way of the sacred openings associated with these powers.

Another explanation traces the origin of Santa's chimney entrance to the primitive belief that supernatural creatures like elves and fairies enter houses through chimneys. It is no coincidence, in this view, that "A Visit from St. Nicholas" calls Santa "a right jolly old elf."

Other elements of pagan religion and of life among the people of northern Europe can reasonably be connected with Santa's chimney. However, historical evidence tying these elements directly to Santa's unconventional mode of visiting us is lacking. Lovers of history may be frustrated, but lovers of myth and lore still enjoy engaging in speculation.

9. Where does the Christmas tree come from?

Perhaps from a millennia-old reverence for trees.
Ancient peoples of many lands considered woods and trees sacred. We learn from the Romans, for example, that the ancient Celts and Germans worshiped the woods, or, rather, perhaps, the divine forces that invigorated and inhabited the woods. Evergreens have over the centuries been thought to possess particular vitality and power, for they survive and even flourish when deprived of warmth and sunlight.

Early Christian legends, too, speak of trees miraculously blossoming in the dead of winter to honor Jesus' birth.

We first hear of *Christmas* trees, however, in the sixteenth century A.D., in Alsace, which at that time was part of the German cultural world. Our first evidence of decorated trees appears in a 1605 entry in a diary from Strasbourg, Alsace's principal city. It would certainly be fair to give the Alsatians the prize for inventing the Christmas tree.

But were the first Christmas trees in Alsace somehow descended from the trees ancient pagans revered? Were the Alsatian trees intended to commemorate the trees that in Christian legend celebrated the Nativity with unseasonable splendor? Did the Alsatians somehow mix these two traditions? Or did they institute something unprecedented? Unless new evidence comes to light, we cannot know for certain.

We do know more about the subsequent popularity of the Christmas tree, though. In the late eighteenth century, the Christmas tree spread throughout much of the German-speaking world, though the custom of having a tree seems to have been confined to the well-to-do. The precise appearance of the tree varied, and we even hear of trees hung upside down! The popularity of the tree in Germany accelerated in the nineteenth century, especially in Protestant regions, with the legend that Martin Luther was the inventor of the Christmas tree very likely playing a role. Much of non-German-speaking Europe adopted the tree as well.

The British royal family deserves much of the credit for establishing the custom of the Christmas tree in England. The family had been decorating Christmas trees since the early 1800s, not surprising since the Hanoverian dynasty had German roots. But it was not until 1848, when an illustration of Queen Victoria's and Prince Albert's Christmas tree was published in the *Illustrated London News,* that England's burgeoning middle class began to imitate the royal couple in large numbers.

The first verifiable references we have to Christmas trees in the United States date from the first third of the nineteenth century, and are connected with German-influenced Pennsylvania. German immigrants apparently brought the custom with them. By 1823, a social group called the Society of Bachelors in York, Pennsylvania, was promising that their tree would be "Superb, superfine, superfrostical, schockagastical, double refined"! (Despite stories that trace the first American Christmas trees back to Hessian mercenaries who fought in the Revolutionary War, Hessians played a minor role, if any, in promoting the Christmas tree in America. We hear virtually nothing about the trees in the United States until more than thirty years after the war.)

In the latter two thirds of the nineteenth century, the custom of decorating Christmas trees spread throughout America, largely due to appealing depictions in influential magazines and other literature. Americans traveling in Europe also brought back to their friends compelling descriptions of German Christmas trees and not infrequently introduced the custom into their own homes. The year 1852 brought the ultimate verification of the acceptance of the Christmas tree as a seasonal tradition in America when Mark Carr set up the first American Christmas tree lot in New York City. We have been visiting tree lots at Christmas ever since.

As in Europe, however, not all Christians had a Christmas tree by the end of the nineteenth century. Some groups and individuals opposed the tree—in 1883 an editor in *The New York Times* referred to it as "a rootless and lifeless corpse." Still others were not able to cut themselves trees or afford to buy them.

In one respect, though, the American Christmas tree was different from others—size. In Europe, the Christmas tree was generally either a very small tree or just a treetop and was placed on a table, as was the tree in the famous 1848 illustration of the British royal family's tree. Americans, in contrast, brought full-sized trees into their homes, often trees extending from the floor to the ceiling. This larger tree, in turn, is now a tradition in homes in many parts of the world.

10. Why do holly and ivy appear at Christmas?

ecause they are green and alive.
Winter can be gloomy. Dusk comes early, and night is long. It is still dark when we rise next morning. Grass is sparse, dull, often brown, and the leaves that surround us with their lush, comforting green in other seasons are long gone. Our world appears lifeless.

The greenery that thrives in these dark days reminds us that even winter is not such a dead time of year after all and that all life has not been extinguished. Intellectually, we may know this, but our spirits are very often in need of something visible and palpable to carry us through to the warm, thriving, green seasons.

Holly and ivy fit the bill perfectly. In winter, they are both green, and holly actually bears bright red berries as well. And so, since late antiquity, Christians have decorated their homes and churches at Christmas with these cheerful symbols of the continuity and renewal of life.

The idea of using festive greens was not Christian in origin, however. For centuries before the birth of Christ, pagans decorated their altars, temples, and sanctuaries with all sorts of greenery and flowers for celebrations. For winter festivities, the Romans, too, used those plants that resist the cold.

Even after the Roman Empire had been Christianized, many people continued to decorate their homes and houses of worship with winter greenery, and the custom gradually became part of the Christian celebration of Christmas. Not without debate, though, as some in the church argued that this pagan practice was idolatrous and should be stamped out. Others, including Pope Gregory the Great, thought it perfectly legitimate to employ nature's gifts to honor Christ and enhance the celebration of his birth. The tradition continued.

Christians also found allegorical significance in the plants. One version of the popular and traditional Christmas carol, "The Holly and the Ivy," provides a perfect illustration:

The Holly bears a berry,
As red as any blood
And Mary bore sweet Jesus Christ
To do poor sinners good.

The Holly bears a prickle
As sharp as any thorn
And Mary bore sweet Jesus Christ
On Christmas day in the morn.

The Holly bears a bark
As bitter as any gall
And Mary bore sweet Jesus Christ
For to redeem us all.

Holly should not just cheer us amidst winter's gloom, the carol suggests, it also should remind us of Christ's sacrifice for us. Symbolically, the red of the holly's berries alludes to Jesus' blood, while the prickles of the holly leaves are the thorns of Jesus' crown. And the bitter bark of the holly brings to mind the cross and the fact that, however much to our benefit, Jesus was born to endure a cruel death.

11. Why is mistletoe so potent?

We don't know for certain, but mistletoe's special "power" may well reflect its special place in the lore and cults of pre-Christian Europe.

Kissing under mistletoe seems to have begun in Great Britain. It may be no accident that early Celts and Scandinavians, two peoples for whom mistletoe had particular significance, dominated Britain at various times. We know they left their marks in a variety of ways.

The Druids, who were the Celts' mysterious priests, used mistletoe in their ceremonies. The Roman writer Pliny observed that Druids "consider nothing more sacred than mistletoe and the tree on which it grows, as long as it is an oak tree." Pliny described a druidic ceremony that, if authentic, reflects the Celts' awe of the plant:

> Using the appropriate ritual procedures, they prepare for a sacrifice and a banquet beneath a tree. Then they guide to the scene two white bulls whose horns are bound for the first time. A priest dressed in a white robe climbs the tree and cuts the mistletoe off with a golden scythe. The falling mistletoe is caught in a white cloak. Then, at last, they sacrifice the victims, asking god to make his gift favorable to those to whom he has given it.

As for the Scandinavians . . . in Norse myth mistletoe plays a special, though notorious, role. The god Baldr, son of Odin and Frigg, had dreams that foretold his death. To protect him, his mother, Frigg, asked all of creation to swear never to harm him. Every plant and tree, all metals, rocks, poisons, and animals—everything in creation—took the oath. Except for mistletoe, that is, for Frigg considered the tiny plant too small to pose a threat. For fun, then, the gods would hurl otherwise lethal objects at the presumably invulnerable Baldr and have a good laugh when they bounced off him. The mischievous and malevolent god Loki, however, discovered Baldr's one weakness and procured some mistletoe. He helped the blind god Hod, who was not in on the plot, to shoot mistletoe at Baldr. And so the god died. The power of tiny mistletoe (whose fruit can in fact be toxic) was great indeed.

Tradition and folk practice have attributed a variety of virtues to mistletoe: It provides magical protection to the home, cures illnesses and counteracts poisons, increases fertility, protects from storms and witches, and brings good luck. It is potent stuff.

The Church also may have contributed to mistletoe's peculiar power to compel a kiss. In the Middle Ages, people were encouraged to assemble "Holy Boughs" of evergreens and decorations to hang near the doors of their homes. The parish priest would make the rounds of his village, blessing the boughs and the homes displaying them. As visitors to these homes passed under a bough, they would be welcomed with a hug, a fitting expression of Christian community and love. Eventually a kiss was added to the hug, presumably something more like the modern liturgical kiss of peace than a kiss of passion. Did mistletoe, one of the evergreens included in the bough, manage to survive the demise of the tradition of the bough *and* carry along with it a somewhat transformed kissing custom?

Alas, no definitive evidence links kissing under mistletoe directly to pagan precedents or to the Holy Bough. It may be a descendent of either, or, in some complex way, of both. Still, there is something special about mistletoe—we don't kiss under holly or ivy, plants that also thrive in winter. And it is difficult to dismiss the ancient reverence for and apprehension about the plant—not to mention its myriad magical powers.

12. Whose idea was it to display Christmas Nativity scenes?

*F*rancis of Assisi may not have set up the first Nativity scene, but he's responsible for making them part of the Christmas celebration.

In December 1223, Francis summoned a good friend named John and asked him to create a palpable reminder of the humility of Christ's birth—a Nativity scene—complete with manger, ox and lamb, and hay. John did as he was asked. Near the Italian village of Greccio, he assembled a manger. On Christmas Eve, villagers provided candles and torches to illuminate the scene. Hay was laid, and a living ox and ass were led to stand as part of the scene. The brothers in Francis' religious order sang hymns by the manger and celebrated a mass during which Francis preached, often referring to Jesus as the "Child of Bethlehem." At the end of the service, we are told, everyone went home filled with joy.

Thomas of Celano, a contemporary of Francis and one of his followers, is our source for this story. Oddly enough, although Celano is explicit about the manger, animals, and hay, he does not mention anyone playing the part of Mary, Joseph, or even Jesus! A story Celano tells, however, seems to suggest that a statue of Jesus was lying in the manger. On that Christmas Eve in Greccio, he says, a man saw a vision of a lifeless child lying in the manger. In the vision, St. Francis went up to the child and wakened it, as if from sleep. Celano tells this story to suggest that Francis had reminded those present—and us, ultimately—that they had forgotten Jesus the child and the significance of his birth. The story also suggests that a "lifeless" child—that is, a statue of baby Jesus—was probably present. What of Mary and Joseph? Some later accounts of that Christmas include them, but we cannot be certain whether they were part of the scene on December 24, 1223.

Celano tells us the hay from Francis' first Nativity scene was kept and proved to have miraculous powers. Sick animals became well after eating the hay. And, most appropriately, contact with the Christmas hay enabled women enduring a difficult labor to give birth easily.

Ironically, as the popularity of Nativity scenes spread, so did their splendor and elaboration. (Some museums today have in their collections Nativity figures, often Italian in origin, of great size, value, and artistic quality.) This is clearly not what Francis had in mind. Celano tell us that Francis re-created the Nativity to remind viewers of the absence of even basic amenities at Christ's birth; the tableau emphasized poverty and humility.

If you'd like to experience something akin to what the locals did in 1223, travel to Greccio, near Riete in Italy, December 24 or 26. On those days, the Franciscan Convento di Greccio attempts to re-create Francis' original Nativity scene. At other times of the year at the Convento, you can visit the Chapel of the Presepio (Chapel of the Crib), which is carved out of the rock, and St. Francis' quarters there.

13. Why are candles so much a part of Christmas?

*I*n part, simply because Christmas occurs at the darkest time of the year.

Everyone notices that the length of the day, and hence the amount of light, waxes and wanes throughout the year. Today we understand why this is the case, and although we might find the shorter days depressing, we don't find them alarming. Ancient peoples in pre-scientific societies, however, became both depressed *and* unsettled. For most of them the sun was a mysterious force, a god, really, of incredible importance—essentially, the source of all light, warmth, and life itself. And yet this god was beyond their understanding and control. They knew, of course, that gods don't *have* to do anything, including warm the earth for our benefit, and as the days became shorter they naturally feared that the sun might disappear.

The most troubling moment in the sun's annual odyssey was the winter solstice. As winter came on, days became ever shorter and sunlight less, temperatures dropped, and nature ceased, for the most part, to grow. For a few days at the solstice (the word is from Latin meaning, "the sun stands still"), the sun seemed to pause, almost as if it was delaying, perhaps even pondering whether it should bother to help us.

What were they to make of this? What if, they wondered, this year the sun just kept retreating until there was no daylight at all? What were they to *do* about this?

Supplying their own light seemed to be a reasonable response. On the most mundane level, December was pretty dark, and human-made light would help everyone see and function better. The ancients also instinctively seemed to know that darkness darkens the human spirit and that light gives what we today call a psychological lift. At the same time, lighting bonfires, lanterns, and candles as both a tribute and a plea to the sun might encourage it not to depart for good—cheer it on to shine again, so to speak.

And so, many ancient religions monitored the waxing and waning of the sunlight as best they could and devised strategies to influence the sun to return. And every year, as the sunlight began to wax again, artificial illumination was also the most appropriate means to celebrate the coming revival of nature and thank the sun for not deserting them.

Early Christians too employed candles for illumination and decoration. Yule logs and bonfires ultimately became an indispensable part of Christmastide. A few Christian writers caviled about pagan precedents, but this was another battle they were destined to lose. And rightly so. Early Christian communities had evening services that required illumination, particularly when Christianity spread to northern climes with their exceedingly dark winters; candles were simply functional. Moreover, it was argued, both the Old and New Testaments repeatedly associate God with light. And so candles were a perfectly appropriate way to honor Jesus, the "light for revelation to the Gentiles and for glory to your people Israel" (Luke 2:32), one who was revealed to humankind through the light of a star.

The Nativity

14. Where does the traditional Christmas narrative come from?

Principally, from the New Testament Gospels of Matthew and Luke.

People who have not spent much time reading and comparing the four Gospels of Matthew, Mark, Luke, and John are sometimes surprised to learn that Mark says nothing of Jesus' birth and that John simply notes that "the Word became flesh" (1:14). Even more surprising, perhaps, the two evangelists who do tell the story of the Nativity tell it very differently. A brief reference chart details some of the most noteworthy differences:

Matthew	*Luke*
Provides a genealogy of Jesus' family	Provides genealogy *after* the Nativity narrative (3:23–38)
Has no story about Elizabeth and Zechariah	The angel Gabriel announces to Zechariah that his wife Elizabeth (Mary's kinswoman) will bear a son named John (the later Baptist)
An unnamed angel appears to *Joseph* to tell him that Mary will have a child from the Holy Spirit	Gabriel appears to *Mary* to tell her that she will have a baby (the Annunciation)
No Visitation	The Visitation (Mary goes to see her kinswoman Elizabeth)
No Magnificat	The Magnificat, Mary's famous song of joy

No mention of a census	The Roman census compels Joseph and a pregnant Mary to go from Nazareth in Galilee to Bethlehem in Judea
Jesus is born in Bethlehem	*Jesus is born in Bethlehem*
No mention of a manger; no story about booked-up inns	Jesus is laid in a manger, for there is no room at the inn
No shepherds	An angel, accompanied by a heavenly host, announces the birth of Christ to shepherds
Still no shepherds	The shepherds find and worship Jesus
The magi come following the Star of Bethlehem; Herod interviews them	No magi, no Star, no Herod
The magi find baby Jesus and give him frankincense, myrrh, and gold	The Nativity narrative ends
The Flight to Egypt: an angel tells Joseph to flee to Egypt until Herod is dead	Includes no Flight to Egypt
The Slaughter of the Innocents: Herod has all boys two years and younger in the neighborhood of Bethlehem slain	Includes no Slaughter of the Innocents
At Herod's death, an angel tells Joseph to bring his family back from Egypt; he does so	Includes no return from Egypt

What are we to make of these discrepancies? From as early as the third century, some Christians have believed that Matthew's and Luke's versions complement each other, each providing different but equally factual elements of the story. Put all the elements together, "harmonize" them in this view, and you have a relatively detailed and historically accurate narrative of what happened.

An old theory maintains that the two versions represent, essentially, the recollections of different witnesses. Since Luke's account, for example, emphasizes Mary's role to a much greater degree, it has been thought to derive from Mary herself—her version of the events, you might say.

Still others claim that Matthew and Luke did not—nor did they intend to—give a factual narrative of Christ's actual birth. Rather, the elements of the two stories are included for thematic, theological reasons and are intended to explain to the reader the significance, not the details, of Christ's birth.

In any event, the popular reaction is often simply to blend the two stories. It is not uncommon, for example, for writers and parents telling the story to have both the shepherds and the magi visit Jesus. What Matthew and Luke would make of this merging of their two versions, we simply don't know.

15. Were they wise men or kings?

*N*either, *actually.*

The Gospel of Matthew, originally written in Greek as was all of the New Testament, speaks of magi from the east visiting the Christ child. In Luke's Gospel, only shepherds come to pay homage.

Some have interpreted the word magi as "wise men." Others have interpreted the magi of Matthew's gospel to be "kings." The issue, then, is what does the word magi really mean?

Medieval and Renaissance kings might have been disappointed to discover that the biblical magi have nothing to do with royalty. "Wise Men" is closer, but, sadly for wise folk everywhere, isn't quite right either. Ancient sources indicate pretty clearly that at the time of the Nativity magi were men who were involved in one way or another with the occult. The English word "magic" is a distant cousin to the Greek word magi. Uh-oh! Magicians bringing gifts? No need for pious Christians to be distressed, though, as we shall see.

The vast majority of people living in the Roman Empire believed in magic of one form or another. The world was full of people making a living from casting spells, providing magical protection, and predicting the future. Even if you had lost faith in your neighborhood palm reader, you most likely had complete faith in your forehead-wrinkle reader's ability to tell your fortune. Of all the professions connected with predicting the future, though, the most respected by far was astrology, whose practice at that time was not distinguished from astronomy. In fact, astrologers were so respected as scientists that the Latin word *mathematicus* could be applied both to mathematicians and astrologers alike. The fact that the gospel's magi identified the star suggests that they were astrologer/astronomers and thus practitioners of a prestigious profession that combined science and religion. Who better to spot such a star? That it was magi, these astrologer/astronomer/priests, who first paid homage to Jesus struck some early Christians as particularly significant. Through the magi, pagan magic yielded to Christ. And since the magi were almost certainly Gentiles, their homage could be seen to symbolize Jesus' mission to all the world.

But how were the magi promoted to kings when there is nothing whatsoever about kings in the Gospels? The beginning of the answer lies not in the New Testament, as we might expect, but in the Old Testament, where Psalm 72:10–11 proclaims:

> May the *kings* of Tarshish and of the isles render him tribute, may the *kings* of Sheba and Seba bring gifts. May all *kings* fall down before him, all nations give him service.

And here is what the early Christian mind, always hunting for references in the Old Testament to Jesus as Messiah, did with that passage: "Let's see, now, in Psalm 72 kings of *three* named places bring gifts . . . Matthew's Gospel mentions *three* gifts brought to the newborn Jesus . . . The kings of Psalm 72 will pay homage . . . The magi of Matthew's Gospel pay homage and, yes, with *three* gifts...Bingo! Those magi in Matthew's Gospel must be the fulfillment of the prophesy of Psalm 72. The magi are kings! What could be more appropriate than kings coming to worship the King of kings?" And so, as early as around 200 A.D., we have evidence of Christians equating the magi with kings.

Not surprisingly, once the pious imagination had crowned the magi as kings, European royals enthusiastically embraced the vision, henceforth able to claim that their counterparts were there with Jesus at the very beginning— that royals, naturally, were those who first bore witness to the birth of the Savior. (Remember, Matthew doesn't mention any shepherds.) And in a world where secular and ecclesiastical nobles were the principal patrons of high art, it was natural for artists to depict Jesus, Mary, and Joseph surrounded by nobles. Besides, what medieval or Renaissance artist could resist depicting exotic potentates in colorful, dazzling robes? And so, when we visit museums and see wonderful depictions of the Nativity, we often see kings in splendid garb paying homage to Jesus.

16. Have modern astronomers identified the Star of Bethlehem?

*N*o, but they're trying.

There are, essentially, three theories about the Star of Bethlehem. According to the first, the star actually existed, but it was an exceptional sign God sent just to mark and announce the Nativity. As such it was a miracle outside the rules of astronomy and science. Once the star had served its function, it disappeared. Don't bother looking for it.

The second theory argues that there was, in fact, no star at all. Matthew included it in his Gospel, the only New Testament mention of the star, to offer a fulfillment to an Old Testament prophecy in Numbers 24:17:

> I see him, but not now;
> I behold him, but not near—
> a star shall come out of Jacob,
> and a scepter shall rise out of Israel.
> it shall crush the borderlands of Moab,
> and the territory of all the Shethites.

Advocates of this approach suggest that the Gospels are not historically accurate, nor were they intended to be. They should be read, rather, for their theological, not their historical, truth. The conclusion is, again, don't bother looking for the star.

The third view assumes that the star not only existed but was a perfectly natural astronomical event. Matthew's depiction of the event may be quite different from how a modern astronomer would report the phenomenon, but it is nonetheless an essentially accurate depiction of the ancient *perception* of an actual event. Now, let's look for it!

The problem is that astronomers have not been able to agree upon what astronomical event it is that Matthew's Gospel portrays. For centuries scientists and other observers have tried to identify it, with the debate becoming particularly intense in recent years.

A brief and only partial list of candidates for the star includes a comet, the planet Venus, a nova, a supernova, a conjunction of planets, an apparent pause in planetary orbit, or some combination of the above.

Even Halley's comet has been considered, although its appearance in 12 B.C. is almost certainly too early for Christ's birth. The great pioneer of Renaissance painting, Giotto, who himself had probably seen Halley's comet in 1301, painted it as the Star of Bethlehem in his marvelous "Adoration of the Magi" fresco in the Scrovegni Chapel in Padua, Italy. Bad astronomy, but great art.

I am not a scientist by a long shot and must confess that I am incapable of evaluating the quality of the different theories, despite considerable research. And so I suggest that if you wish to explore the debate, you start with Mark Kidger's 1999 book, *The Star of Bethlehem*, which provides an up-to-date and accessible survey of opinions.

Perhaps the most striking thing about the search for the Star of Bethlehem is that in our secular, skeptical age, the passion to find historical truth in an account of faith burns as hot as ever. And it is the scientists who are doing the looking.

17. What are frankincense and myrrh, anyway?

hey are precious resins that in the ancient world were used in a variety of surprising ways.

In the ancient world, you could make a great deal of money selling frankincense and myrrh, but it wasn't easy. To obtain the resins, you would have to travel to Southern Arabia or to the horn of Africa, where you would find the frankincense tree, the *boswellia sacra,* and the myrrh tree, the *commiphora myrrha* (which actually resembles a bush more than a tree). Harvesting resins from these trees was not unlike tapping maple trees for syrup. You would strip the bark, cut into the wood, and then wait for the trees to bleed the liquid, which ultimately turned into the desired resins. Then you would bring the resins back to Mediterranean markets.

The difficulty of obtaining frankincense and myrrh meant that the supply was limited. At the same time, the variety and importance of their uses kept the demand high. As a result of high demand and low supply, frankincense and myrrh were quite expensive.

Frankincense was a critical ingredient in the incense and oils used in the Temple in Jerusalem, but pagans also exploited its fragrance in incense, oils, and perfumes, and used it even to mask the repugnant fumes of bodies being cremated. Myrrh was employed as an aromatic additive as well.

The Bible suggests that both substances could also find their way into the bedroom. The Song of Songs repeatedly makes the erotic connection unambiguously, and in Proverbs a woman bent on seduction tells her intended victim, "I have perfumed my bed with myrrh, aloes, and cinnamon. Come, let us take our fill of love until morning . . . For my husband is not at home" (7:17–19).

Frankincense and myrrh are most famous, though, as the gifts, along with gold, that the magi brought to the newborn Jesus. From very early on, Christians have commented on the suggestiveness of these gifts. Two of them seem to fulfill a prophecy in Isaiah 60:6: "A multitude of camels shall cover you, the young camels of Midian and Ephah; all those from Sheba shall come. They shall bring gold and frankincense, and shall proclaim the praise of the Lord."

All three were precious commodities, clearly fit for a king. Gold was the metal most closely associated with royalty. Frankincense's association with the Jewish Temple priesthood could be symbolic of Jesus' priesthood, or even of his divinity.

Both frankincense and myrrh were used to treat wounds, and modern scientific research has shown that myrrh has genuine antiseptic and analgesic properties. And, in fact, according to Mark's Gospel, on the cross Jesus was offered wine laced with myrrh to temper his pain. Myrrh was also used to anoint the dead, just as John's Gospel tells us Jesus was embalmed with myrrh after his crucifixion (19:39–40). Myrrh, then, foreshadows Christ's suffering and death.

We who are accustomed to seeing nothing but joy in the Nativity accounts and their commemoration at Christmas may be surprised, even a bit disturbed, by this somber suggestion of the crucifixion. Through the ages, however, Christians contemplating and depicting the Nativity have been very conscious of the fact that its meaning for them is principally as a prelude—a precondition, one might say—to the crucifixion and resurrection. Renaissance painters of the Nativity and of Madonna and Child scenes, for example, frequently depict Mary as lost in melancholy. She knows what horrors await her son.

18. Who was Herod?

*H*erod the Great ruled Judea from 40 B.C. until his death in 4 B.C. The Gospels tell us that Jesus was born during his reign and that he tried to have the infant Jesus murdered.

Herod had remarkable vision and political instincts, but he was also unscrupulous and ruthless. He recognized that the will of the Romans determined who would rule in Judea, and he did a remarkable job of gaining and keeping Roman patronage. In 40 B.C., Mark Antony and Octavian (the future emperor Augustus, in whose reign Jesus was born) convinced the Roman Senate to name Herod King of Judea. With Roman support, he was able to overcome considerable resistance and by the end of 37 B.C. controlled much of what today is Israel and Palestine.

The Romans had given Herod his kingship, and he knew they could just as easily take it away. Maintaining good personal and political relations with Rome's leaders was absolutely critical to preserving his position, but they were a difficult bunch to deal with. For example, Mark Antony was, early on, Herod's principal Roman ally, but the Egyptian queen Cleopatra, Antony's mistress, wanted Herod's kingdom. If that threat weren't enough, according to Herod's lost memoirs, Cleopatra also tried to seduce him! He had to resist both the temptation to accept the dazzling Cleopatra's advances and also the temptation, he tells us, to have her assassinated. And yet Herod managed to survive in this delicate and dangerous situation. And later, when Octavian defeated Antony and Cleopatra, Herod again survived, even though he had supported the losing side.

Not surprisingly, Herod's palace was full of intrigue and tragedy. He executed his uncle, his mother-in-law, his beloved wife Mariamme (Lord Byron wrote a poem about Herod's agonized regret after the fact, "Herod's Lament for Mariamme"), three of his sons, and one of his barbers. The emperor Augustus joked, "I'd rather be Herod's pig than his son," alluding both to Herod's savagery and to Jewish abstention from pork.

Herod is best known these days, though, as the man who ordered the slaughter of the little boys of Bethlehem in an attempt to kill Jesus. Even though this act, known as the Slaughter of the Innocents, seems to fit into Herod's modus operandi, some historians and theologians doubt whether the incident actually occurred. They note that the ancient Jewish historian Josephus, who left us a reasonably detailed account of Herod's last years, does not mention the Slaughter, even though something so monstrous would have been impossible to leave out. No other ancient source testifies unambiguously to the Slaughter. Those who believe that it actually occurred argue that Bethlehem was a small town and that infant mortality was very high in the ancient world—and so the number of boys slain would not have been so high, perhaps even fewer than twenty. According to this view, the murder of so few children, though noteworthy, could easily have been left out of accounts of Herod's otherwise very eventful and colorful life.

Herod was also a great builder, and he left his mark on Judea's architecture. We can still see the considerable remains of many of his projects, and a tour of Herodian monuments is a fascinating way to spend a week. Among the highlights are Masada, his lofty mountaintop fortress palace; the Herodium, another spectacular fortress palace, which also served as his tomb; and Caesarea, the seaside town that Herod transformed into one of the most important and luxurious ports of the eastern Mediterranean (it also contains Crusader ruins). The excavations of these and other sites provide a wonderful look into the career of the king and life in his kingdom.

19. When was Jesus born?

ery likely some time around 5 B.C., but we simply don't know for certain.

At the recent turn of the millennium, many Christians celebrated the two-thousandth anniversary of Jesus' birth. This anniversary was based upon a very old, but almost certainly incorrect, estimate of the year of his birth. How this miscalculation came to be is a fascinating story.

In 525 A.D., Pope John I asked an abbot named Dionysius Exiguus (in English, "Dionysius the Small") to calculate the date of Easter in the coming year. Dionysius did that, but far more important in the process he also established the system of counting the years that we still use today.

Until then, Easter had been calculated according to a calendar whose year 1 was the first year of the Emperor Diocletian's reign (284 A.D.). In that system, what we today know as 294 A.D. was the year 10; 299 A.D. was the year 15; and so on. But Diocletian was remembered in Dionysius' day as one of Christianity's most brutal persecutors, and the pious abbot was unhappy that the career of such a man was honored by providing the starting point for the enumeration of the years. And so, Dionysius simply designated the year of Jesus' birth as year 1 and labeled all subsequent years *anni Domini nostri* ("years of our Lord"), the Latin phrase that gives us the "A.D." common today. ("B.C." is a much later invention.) In one stroke, the good abbot had renumbered the calendar!

Unfortunately, Dionysius' calculation of Christ's birth year was flawed. For example, he designated the first year "year 1," when it should have been "year 0." We can't blame him for this problem—the Romans had no zero.

So, in what year was Jesus born?

The sources make it extremely difficult to be sure. Here is just one of the problems involved:

The Gospel of Matthew implies that Jesus was born shortly before King

Herod's death, which probably occurred in 4 B.C. This seems to suggest that Jesus was likely born in 5, or perhaps 6, or even 4 B.C. Luke's Gospel, however, tells us that the famous census of the Emperor Augustus was taken when Quirinius was governor of Syria (Luke 2:1–2). We know that Quirinius became governor of Syria in 6 A.D. There thus seems to be a *ten-year gap* between Matthew's and Luke's evidence for the dating of Jesus' birth! (Arguments are also made for several years between 4 B.C. and 6 A.D., and even for years earlier than 6 B.C.)

Various attempts have been made to bridge or explain this gap, and the issues involved are extremely complicated. One piece of evidence, though, causes many scholars to favor circa 5 B.C. over 6 A.D. and other proposals. Luke's Gospel (3:1, 23) tells us that Jesus began his public ministry when he was *about thirty* years old in the fifteenth year of the Emperor Tiberius' reign, that is, 27–28 A.D. If we count back, that would put us in 3 or 2 B.C. The wiggle room that Luke's word "about" provides makes it easy to imagine that Jesus was born in 5 or 4 B.C., and thus began his ministry when he was perhaps thirty-one or thirty-two, ages that certainly qualify as "about thirty." A birth year of 6 A.D., though, would suggest that Jesus was twenty-one or twenty-two when he started his public ministry. That hardly seems to fit "about thirty."

The millennium we all observed when the calendar turned to 2000 was most probably not really the second millennium of Christ's birth. It would have actually been better designated as "Dionysius' Millennium," since it was really a creation of the abbot's revolutionary calendar.

20. What do the ox and ass have to do with Jesus' birth?

hey are excellent examples of how early Christians searched in the Old Testament for foreshadowings of Christ's birth, but they do not appear in the Gospel narratives.

Since early Christians believed (as do Christians today) that Jesus was the Messiah promised by the God of the Old Testament, they searched for allusions to him in the Old Testament. But how to do this? The Old Testament is, in fact, many texts, and all together a formidable tome. How does one start?

If they had had our technology, they probably would have started out by doing computer word searches. Using the Nativity accounts of Matthew and Luke, they would have typed in key words, names, and phrases, such as *census, Bethlehem, virgin, Joseph, birth*. The computer would have directed them to Old Testament passages in which those words or phrases occur. Then their analysis would have started.

Early Christian writers actually did essentially that, plunging into the Old Testament, looking for these words and phrases, and otherwise searching for passages that might allude to Christ. But it must have taken them an immense amount of time. Those with good memories probably had a considerable catalogue of Old and New Testament words and phrases in their heads, although some of them also would have had the texts nearby for reference.

One such researcher ran into the following quotation in Isaiah 1:3: "The ox knows its owner, and the donkey its master's crib; but Israel does not know, my people do not understand." You can almost picture the light bulb going on above his head—couldn't this master's crib be the manger of Luke's Nativity account?

Many early Christians found this association compelling, and the ox and the donkey even found their way into the very popular Gospel of Pseudo-Matthew, where their adoration of Jesus "fulfilled what had been said by

Isaiah the prophet." (More gospels than Matthew, Mark, Luke, and John were written; but concerns about the others' late dates, authenticity, and/or orthodoxy caused the Church to exclude them from the Bible.) Eventually artists began including the ox and the ass in paintings that depicted Christ's birth. As paintings came to be one of the principal sources of popular notions concerning the Nativity, the ox and the ass became part of the standard narrative and participants in virtually every depiction of the stable and the baby Jesus.

This may not have been the early Christians' intention, though.

Ancient and medieval Christians could be very sophisticated in their use of allegory and symbolism and often interpreted biblical passages in non-literal ways. They may not have expected the Isaiah/Luke "master's crib" association to be taken as part of the Nativity narrative. The point of incorporating the ox and the ass into early depictions of the Nativity was not to suggest that those animals had actually been present at Christ's birth, but rather to remind us that his birth was a fulfillment of Old Testament prophecy. This would make the ox and the ass even more significant, though less historical.

Keep in mind that the search for Old Testament prophecies of Christ as Messiah had the authority of the Gospels themselves. Luke, the only evangelist who mentions the manger, takes pains to incorporate unambiguous references to the Old Testament, not least of all to Isaiah. When they incorporated allusions to Old Testament prophecies into their Nativity narratives, later Christian writers must have thought of themselves simply as following a tradition the evangelists had started.

The Arts and Senses

21. Why did Charles Dickens write A Christmas Carol?

argely for two reasons, each both economic and personal. Dickens wrote his much-beloved work during the third year of a terrible decade in nineteenth-century England, the so-called "hungry forties." Hundreds of thousands of workers were unemployed, and famine was widespread in the North. The high price of bread forced some poor families to decide which of their children to feed based on their relative sickliness and individual odds of survival. Meanwhile, the landed gentry continued to hunt grouse on their estates, and many prosperous industrialists simply shut down their factories, waiting out the economic downturn in their comfortable houses and clubs.

In 1843 the biographer and social critic Thomas Carlyle commented on the misery: "Here at Chelsea, for the first time, I notice the garden palings [slats] torn up this winter and stolen for fuel—a bitter symptom, for the poor in general are very honest." One out of every eleven persons in England and Wales were paupers, according to a March 1842 census, and a series of government reports catalogued the abusive conditions under which those who *did* have jobs labored. In May of that year, one such report on conditions for workers in the mines actually evoked tears from some members of Parliament. Another inspired the poet Elizabeth Barrett Browning to write her famous "A Cry of the Children":

> But the young, young children, O my brothers,
>   Do you ask them why they stand
> Weeping sore before the bosoms of their mothers,
>   In our happy Fatherland?

The second child in a family of eight, Charles Dickens had known financial uncertainty and poverty firsthand in boyhood, but by the 1840s he was a successful writer. Ever sensitive to the hardships confronting the poor, the uneducated, and the downtrodden, Dickens began to contemplate writing a book to deal with their suffering. In September 1843, Dickens visited a "Ragged School," a school where children were in fact warehoused in deplorable conditions. The next month, he spoke at a fund-raising dinner for the Manchester Athenaeum, a charitable cultural institution for the working class. A number of notable and influential people attended, including the politician Richard Cobden and the future prime minister, Benjamin Disraeli. There in impassioned rhetoric, Dickens talked of the appalling conditions he had witnessed and expressed a desire to take his listeners on a tour of the jails and poorhouses he had visited, to force them to confront for themselves the conditions under which their brothers and sisters subsisted.

Despising the way his own class dismissed the sufferings of the poor, Dickens at last determined to write a story that focused on a misanthrope who embodied the callous disregard for others and the poverty of spirit he saw about him—and Ebenezer Scrooge was born. He decided to set the story at Christmas, and, once back in London from Manchester, set to work immediately.

His haste was personally motivated as well, for, in truth, Dickens needed money. Despite the wild popularity of his previous works, sales for the early installments of his most recent novel, *Martin Chuzzlewit*, had fallen far below expectations, and Dickens' publishers were considering decreasing his monthly stipend of £200 to £150. Even while supporting a wife and four children (with a fifth on the way), Dickens continued to be plagued by the demands of his father and other relatives for financial assistance. "He and all of them look upon me as something to be plucked," the beleaguered author reported.

Once begun, *A Christmas Carol* engaged its writer as few other projects had. "I was very much affected by the little Book myself," Dickens observed to a friend, and became "reluctant to lay it aside for a moment." Dickens' care over *A Christmas Carol* shows in the manuscript draft—now housed in the Berg Collection of the New York Public Library—which reveals how thoroughly he read over and revised the text again and again, making myriad changes, additions, and deletions. Sent to the printers late in November, the book was ready for the public in time for Christmas.

It was a prodigious success. The first printing of six thousand copies sold out in a matter of days. By the end of the year, nearly fifteen thousand copies had been purchased. The popular and critical response was virtually unanimous in its praise. The poet Thomas Hood described the novel as "a happy inspiration of the heart that warms every page. It is impossible to read, without a glowing bosom and burning cheeks, between love and shame for our kind." "Who can listen to objections regarding such a book as this?" the sometimes acerbic novelist and reviewer William Makepeace Thackeray wrote in *Fraser's Magazine.* "It seems to me a national benefit, and to every man or woman who reads it a personal kindness."

And what of Dickens' financial burdens? Sadly, initial sales of *A Christmas Carol* did little to lighten them. Angered by his perception that his publishers were losing faith in his work, Dickens had insisted on paying for the production of *A Christmas Carol* himself. The agreement allowed Dickens to take all profits after paying a commission to the publishers on copies sold. Dickens himself had supervised the production of the little volume, ordering elaborate binding and gilding. Nevertheless, he required that the price be set at no more than five shillings, hoping that as many readers as possible might buy the work. The expense of production and the relatively low price probably cost Dickens the large return he had been expecting. In February 1844, counting on profits of at least £1,000, Dickens discovered he had realized less than twenty percent of that estimate.

In the long run, however, *A Christmas Carol* enriched Dickens as much as or more than any other work of his career. A perennial favorite of readers to this day, it was also a favorite among Dickens' audiences and a staple of the wildly popular and lucrative readings Dickens gave in his tours of England and America. By most estimates, Dickens earned about £45,000 from his readings, this total amounting to almost half the estate he left at his death. The little Christmas book, then, contributed in no small way to Dickens' financial legacy—the material security he labored to give his children. Its greater legacy, of course, is ours to share year after year.

22. Was Ebenezer Scrooge based on anyone in particular?

*G*abriel *Grub was his name, in fact, and he was a grave* digger who was visited by goblins! Dickens had created a prototype for Scrooge in a tale titled "The Story of the Goblins who Stole a Sexton." In that story, Dickens wrote about a grouchy grave digger and sexton "who eyed each merry face as it passed him by, with such a deep scowl of malice and ill-humour, as it was difficult to meet without feeling something the worse for."

On his way to dig a grave on Christmas Eve—an appropriate seasonal activity for a man who associated Christmas cheer with "measles, scarlet-fever, thrush, hooping-cough"—Grub heard a boy singing a Christmas song. He cheered himself up by striking the child on the head with his lantern five or six times. He then proceeded to the graveyard, and when he'd completed his digging, he sat on a tombstone to drink from his flask and laughed, "Ho! Ho! A coffin at Christmas—a Christmas Box. Ho! Ho! Ho!" A mysterious voice responded, "Ho! Ho! Ho!" The answering voice belonged to a goblin! A host of goblins appeared before the terrified Grub and leapt over tombstones at an ever-increasing pace until the first goblin, apparently a goblin king, pulled the dizzy grave digger under the earth.

Grub found himself in an underground cave. A thick cloud concealed the back of the cave. When the cloud rolled away, he saw scenes of how others spent Christmas. Grub watched a poor but happy family welcome their father home from work. Then he saw a bedroom where the youngest child lay dying. At the boy's passing, the other children recognized "that he was an angel looking down upon, and blessing them, from a bright and happy Heaven." Grub saw the parents grow old and die, and the surviving grown children go on contentedly and cheerfully, fully confident that the entire family would "one day meet again."

Grub saw other scenes as well, scenes of people courageously persevering amidst the most difficult circumstances. "Above all, he saw that men like himself, who snarled at the mirth and cheerfulness of others, were the foulest weeds on the fair surface of the earth," and he realized that "it was a very decent and respectable sort of world after all." (The king of the goblins aided in his rehabilitation by kicking him a great deal.)

Like Scrooge, he woke up the next day a changed man.

In *A Christmas Carol,* Dickens transformed Grub into Scrooge, the unnamed family on the cave wall into the Cratchits, the dying boy into Tiny Tim (who in the new story is saved), and the goblins into ghosts. We might think it odd to have ghosts and goblins in Christmas stories, but keep in mind that Christmas falls right in the dead of winter, one of the coldest, darkest, bleakest, spookiest times of year. Grub's story first appeared in chapter 28 (chapter 29 in some editions) of *The Posthumous Papers of the Pickwick Club,* about seven years before the publication of *A Christmas Carol* in 1843.

23. Where did the idea for the movie It's a Wonderful Life come from?

*I*t's *Charles Dickens' A Christmas Carol. But in reverse.*
British and American studios have made many film adaptations of the Dickens classic. Even when the story is transferred to the world of cartoon animation—as in, for example, *Mr. Magoo's Christmas Carol*—or when Muppets play the Cratchits, the plot and characters are perfectly recognizable.

Although most viewers are unaware of the link, Frank Capra's *It's a Wonderful Life* is every bit as much a descendent of *A Christmas Carol*. The connection is just not so obvious.

In both stories, on Christmas Eve, supernatural beings (an angel in *Life*, spirits in *Carol*) visit a man of business who is in serious peril. Each man has until now misunderstood the significance of his life and career and needs correcting. Both must review and reassess their past lives (and their possible futures) in order to come to the truth, although neither of them desires to do so. In neither story can the man intervene in the scenes the supernatural beings allow him to see. In both cases, the reassessment brings wisdom, happiness, and salvation.

It is difficult to recognize the parallels between *It's a Wonderful Life* and *A Christmas Carol*, perhaps, because many elements of *Carol* have been cleverly transformed in *Life*. Here are a couple of examples.

George Bailey is really an anti-Scrooge. Scrooge is a financially successful businessman who has in fact squandered his life. Bailey is a businessman who is apparently a failure but has in fact accomplished a great deal. Each has to review his life in order to understand what success really means.

Since George Bailey is a generous, decent man, he's no Scrooge. But how can you have a version of *A Christmas Carol* without Scrooge? Well, you can't. And so another character, Mr. Potter, is the Scrooge of the story. In his wealth, age, loneliness, bitterness, coldness, ruthlessness—I could go on and on—Potter is in fact a very close cousin to Scrooge.

What about the Cratchits? Here, the movie offers another clever twist. The Baileys, with their dilapidated house, broken-down car, and perpetual struggles to make ends meet, fit the bill. George Bailey, moreover, like Bob Cratchit, is overworked but getting (in material terms) nowhere. Despite all this, until disaster strikes George on Christmas Eve, the Bailey family is full of the same kind of warmth and solidarity that readers find in the Cratchits. (There is even a sick child in *Life*, although Zu Zu's illness is trivial compared to Tiny Tim's.)

The endings of the two tales are mirror images of each other. After realizing the true meaning of life—and of *their* lives—both Ebenezer and George are overwhelmed by gratitude and joy. But *Carol* ends with an enlightened Ebenezer doing deeds of generosity, whereas *Life* ends with an enlightened George *receiving* (at last!) generosity.

Frank Capra and his screenwriters deserve a great deal of credit for this brilliant adaptation of Dickens' novel. But the idea for *It's a Wonderful Life* actually came from a short story titled "The Greatest Gift," by Philip Van Doren Stern. The movie is different from the short story in some significant ways—Stern's hero, named George *Pratt*, is merely a bank clerk, for example—but the fundamental conceit of the story—a modern, Americanized *Christmas Carol* in which the protagonist realizes the value of his life—is Stern's.

24. What is the origin of the Christmas carol?

The first carols were songs accompanied by dance, and they were not necessarily associated with Christmas at all.

The word *carol* seems to be derived from the French word *carole,* meaning a circle dance. And, in fact, early carols were usually performed as part of a dance or procession. In a sense, when modern carolers go from house to house singing, they are echoing what medieval carolers did.

The earliest carols, in the Middle Ages, could treat virtually any topic. Politics and love, for example, were appropriate themes, and the lyrics could even be bawdy. But Christmas was a season particularly full of revelry, song, and dance. And so, over time, Christmas carols came to be the predominant type of carol. The result is that when someone mentions a carol these days, most of us naturally, and for our era, correctly, think only of Christmas songs.

The Church may have promoted Christmas' assimilation of the carol as well. Many of the prominent pagan religions of Europe incorporated dance accompanied by song into their worship, including their solstice rites, the rites with which the Christian celebration of Christmas competed. This was at least one of the reasons why the early Church was generally opposed to dance, particularly in religious contexts. Some Church leaders railed against dancing; others, recognizing the powerful hold so many pre-Christian customs retained, decided to co-opt music and dance. And so it is not out of the question that some members of the clergy may have provided religious lyrics for popular, secular carol melodies or composed entirely new carols in an effort to reform or redirect the sometimes bawdy, often raucous winter singing and dancing. Over time, the dancing declined, and seasonal Christian themes came to predominate.

A valid but oversimplified way of looking at the difference between early carols and hymns would be that the carols, whatever their theme, were performed on the streets and in homes, whereas hymns were performed in churches and monasteries in liturgical contexts. Carols belonged to the people, one might say, but this does not mean that they were a form of folk music composed by the common people, though they could contain genuine folk elements. In fact, many carols show clear signs of formal education, while in the Middle Ages most people were illiterate.

One indication of this education is that quite a few of the early carols are macaronic—that is, their lyrics are composed of a mixture of both English and Latin. Here's an example (the original is on the left; on the right I've modernized some of the English spelling and translated the Latin):

original	*modern*
Vpon a nyght an aungell bright	Upon a night an angel bright
Pastoribus apparuit,	To shepherds appeared,
And anone right thurgh Goddes myght	And at once through God's might
Lux magna illis claruit.	A great light shone on them
For loue of vs (Scripture seith thus)	For love of us (Scripture says thus)
Nunc natus est Altissimus	Now the Exalted One is born

It is also possible to see the hand of the clergy in the composition of many carols. Again, Latin lyrics may be a clue. As a story about the great British playwright, Ben Jonson, shows, the clergy above all others were associated with the ability to read Latin:

In 1598, Ben Jonson was on trial for murder but escaped conviction by employing an ingenious legal technicality that would be the envy of any modern pettifogger. At that time in England, the legal definition of a clergyman was someone who could read Latin. And clergy could not be tried for murder. So Jonson demonstrated that he could read Latin in court, thus proving that he was, legally speaking, a clergyman (although by any other definition he most certainly was not). Thereafter, the murder charge was dropped. Jonson did not get off scot-free, though. His property was confiscated, and his thumb was branded with a "T" (for Tyburn, the place where he would have been executed for the murder). Since clergy could invoke this immunity only once—they did not enjoy carte blanche to pile up dozens of victims—the brand would show the authorities that Jonson had already played his get-out-of-jail-free card, should he ever murder again.

25. What does Bilbo Baggins
have to do with Christmas?

J. R. R. Tolkien, the author of The Hobbit *and of* The
Lord of the Rings *trilogy, composed some remarkable Christmas
letters that we can enjoy today. As he created the mythical Middle Earth for
his hero Bilbo Baggins in those novels, Tolkien created in his letters a remarkable
universe for Santa Claus.

Starting in 1920, each Christmas Tolkien would write a letter to his children
from Father Christmas, the British version of Santa Claus. The children
might find the letter in the fireplace, a natural place to leave a letter if you've
entered the house through the chimney. Or it might even arrive with the genuine
mail—Tolkien was able to acquire the cooperation of the local mailman
in the fiction.

And what letters! Tolkien illustrated them copiously himself, sometimes
at the very last minute before Christmas Day, although the letters would
claim that the illustrations were the work of Father Christmas, his elf assistant
Ilbereth, or the North Polar Bear. He took considerable pains to make the
envelopes look authentic (to children's eyes, that is), stamping them with
Polar stamps that depicted Father Christmas or even the North Pole crowned
by the aurora borealis. Markings on the envelopes would indicate the form
of delivery: "By direct Reindeer Post" or "By gnome-carrier."

The contents of the letters are just as delightful as the presentation. They
are essentially reports of what had transpired at the North Pole since last
Christmas. The star of most of the reports is really the mischievous North
Polar Bear, who, though Father Christmas' loyal and beloved assistant, is
constantly causing trouble. (Elves help Father Christmas, but there's no sign
of a Mrs.)

The letters recount a variety of events, such as the destruction of Father
Christmas' old house and the construction of his new one, North Pole celebrations,
and troubles getting everything ready for Christmas.

Even adventures. In one letter, Father Christmas tells of his discovery that Goblins had tunneled into his basement and had been stealing Christmas presents. With the help of the North Polar Bear and the Red Gnomes, he was able to capture some Goblins and get the presents back. But the next year the brazen Goblins returned, and this time they dared to attack his house! Again with the help of Polar Bear and the Gnomes, after about two weeks of fighting Father Christmas was able to kill a great many Goblins and put to rout those that survived.

The letters are notably free of moralizing. Father Christmas appears to be doing nothing more than informing. And although good and evil are presented distinctly and unambiguously, Father Christmas never preaches. And yet we can wonder if the growing menace of the Goblins in the letters from the 1930s reflected awareness of the contemporaneous menace that was to cause World War II.

To our good fortune, Tolkien's daughter-in-law, Baillie Tolkien, edited the letters and published a selection of them, including a great many of the original illustrations. Houghton Mifflin issued a revised edition, titled *The Father Christmas Letters*, in 1999. It is not to be missed.

26. What is the Magnificat?

The Magnificat is the song of joy and hope Mary proclaims in Luke's Gospel when, pregnant with Jesus, she goes to visit her kinswoman Elizabeth. But Magnificats are a wonderful type of Christmas music that Mary's song inspired.

First, Luke's account.

Let's set the scene. Elizabeth had been unable to conceive and was past the age of bearing children. The angel Gabriel appeared to her husband, Zechariah, and told him, "Your wife Elizabeth will bear you a son." When a puzzled Zechariah observed to Gabriel that he and Elizabeth were a bit old to be conceiving children, his skepticism cost him the ability to speak until God's promise was fulfilled. A delighted Elizabeth became pregnant with the future John the Baptist. When Elizabeth was five months pregnant, Gabriel announced to Mary that she would conceive Jesus, the "Son of God." He also informed her that Elizabeth was, contrary to nature but in conformity with God's will, pregnant. It is no surprise that Mary rushed off to visit Elizabeth.

For most of the history of Christianity, this visit has been *the* visit of which Christians speak, and it is called the "Visitation." (It is not to be confused with *the* announcement, that of Gabriel to Mary, which is called the "Annunciation.")

When the kinswomen came together, Elizabeth recognized Mary's condition and that she was carrying the Lord within her. Mary's proclamation in response to Elizabeth is known as the Magnificat. It begins, in the King James translation, as follows:

. . . My soul doth magnify the Lord,
And my spirit hath rejoiced in God my Saviour.
For he hath regarded the low estate of his handmaiden;

for behold, from henceforth all generations shall call me blessed.
For he that is mighty hath done to me great things; and holy *is* his name.
And his mercy is on them that fear him from generation to generation.

(Luke 1:46–50 KJV)

Mary's words are beautiful, powerful, and moving, a consolation to the oppressed and unsettling to the mighty, an ecstatic celebration, for many Christians, of a great historical moment. It is no surprise, then, that many of the world's greatest composers have put Mary's words to music. These musical versions of Mary's Magnificat are, unsurprisingly, also called Magnificats.

It would be difficult to list all the composers who have set Mary's words to music. Let me just recommend three of the most wonderful Magnificats, ones that are often performed at Christmas and are easily available on compact disc: Monteverdi's (from his Vespers of 1610); J. S. Bach's (look for BWV 243 on the label); and Mozart's (from his *Vesperae solennes de confessore*).

But why is Mary's song called the Magnificat? The word *Magnificat* is Latin and means "it magnifies." Yet the historical Mary most probably spoke Aramaic, not Latin. Luke wrote his Gospel in Greek, not Latin. And we who use the term *Magnificat* today speak English (or other modern languages), not Latin. So how did this fourth language, Latin, used by none of the participants (speaker, author, reader), become part of our vocabulary of Christmas?

The first word of the Magnificat Luke wrote in his Gospel is Greek for "it magnifies." Magnificat is, thus, simply a Latin translation of the first word Mary speaks. It is not uncommon for us to remember the first words or lines of songs and poems, even when we've forgotten the title. Many songs—especially Christmas songs—in fact derive their titles from their first lines. And so it makes perfect sense for us to recall Mary's lovely proclamation by its first word.

But why a *Latin* word? For much of the Middle Ages and even in the Renaissance in western Europe, Latin was the language of the law, of literature, and of the Church. Greek was largely lost in the West, and this meant that even literate clergy had to rely on Latin translations for their knowledge of scripture. And so, Christians in Italy, Spain, Germany, England, Ireland, and a host of other countries were completely unacquainted with the Greek in which Luke had actually written. Since for them the Latin translation was *the* authentic scripture, "Magnificat" was also *the* authentic first word of Mary's proclamation and became its title.

When Greek finally came to the West and churchfolk started to study the New Testament in the Greek original, well, it was simply too late. Latin had for so long and so thoroughly dominated the culture of Christianity—including its music—that there was no way Luke's Greek word could unseat the by then familiar Latin, "Magnificat."

And so when you listen to one of the many Magnificats as you sit in a church or concert hall or lie cozily near your Christmas tree, you are most probably hearing Latin sung. But in whatever language you hear it, it is a wonderful song.

WASSAIL

CELEBRATION

27. Why do we celebrate Jesus' birth on December 25?

The date was selected, most probably, so that Christian celebration might compete head-to-head with pagan festivities.

The four Gospels tell us nothing about the date of Jesus' birth. The evangelists either did not know or did not consider the date important. The earliest Christians were expecting the world to end very, very soon, and so they weren't particularly concerned with celebrating, or even identifying, Christ's birthday.

But before too long, Christians came to realize that the Church might remain on earth for quite a while, and the details of Jesus' biography and the way in which Christians would commemorate and celebrate his life became far more important. Unfortunately, no information was at hand to help them figure out the correct date of the Nativity. So they found themselves searching for an answer in that last refuge of all the finest historians, the imagination.

Quite a few dates were proposed, selected mostly for theological or aesthetic reasons. Here's an example of the sort of reasoning they employed:

Step 1: The Bible tells us that on the first day of creation God "separated the light from the darkness" (Genesis 1:4). Step 2: Since God's creation is so perfect and symmetrical, these two parts, light and darkness, must have been equal. Step 3: So, if we wish to find out which day of the year God did this separating, we need a day when light and darkness are of the same length. Step 4: Why, on the vernal equinox the hours of daylight and darkness are the same! The first day of creation, then, must have taken place on the vernal equinox, March 25 (in the ancient Roman calendar). Step 5: The Bible further tells us that God made the sun on the fourth day (Genesis 1:16). That means, using the discovery that the first day of creation was March 25, God made the sun on March 28. Step 6: The Old Testament also tells us that the Messiah will be the "sun of righteousness" (Malachi 4:2).

Step 7: Therefore, Jesus = Sun. Step 8: Bingo! Jesus must have born on the same day that God created the sun—that is, on March 28.

The reasoning behind these calculations strikes us as astonishing, almost comical. But in ancient Rome, Christian and non-Christian thinkers alike tended to schematize both science and history. They looked for neat, symbolic numbers that would appropriately reflect the logic and grandeur of God's plans. An event as momentous as the Savior's arrival simply could not be imagined as happening on any old date. And so they searched for a date by asking, virtually, "If I were God and could choose any date for my son's birth—as God, needless to say, did—which would I choose?" March 28 was just one of many guesses. As was December 25, apparently. With so much competition, then, how did December 25 win out? We don't really know for certain, but here's the most persuasive theory.

Pagans of the Roman Empire celebrated the birthday of Sol Invictus (the "unconquered sun" god) on December 25. Many also identified Sol Invictus with Mithras, a very popular pagan deity who was a formidable rival of Christ's in the crowded marketplace of ancient religions. At some point in the fourth century, the Church decided to compete with Mithraism and with the cult of Sol Invictus by celebrating Christ's birthday on precisely the same day that pagans were celebrating the birth of one of their most popular gods. Not only were the Christians hoping to steal this day (as well as the pagans' hearts and souls) from Mithras, they were also brilliantly co-opting one of the pagans' most beloved holidays.

"You don't want to give up your mid-winter festival by becoming a Christian?" the Church seemed to plead, "And you don't have to! Just celebrate Jesus' birth, instead of Sol Invictus.'" And the plea was remarkably successful.

28. What is the Epiphany?

The Epiphany is the celebration on January 6 of the manifestation of Jesus' divinity. It is also the last of the Twelve Days of Christmas and, so, the official end of the Christmas season.

Most Christians these days simply accept Christ's divinity as fact. In the early Church, though, it was very difficult to get everyone to agree. Some thought it was inconceivable that God would allow himself or his divine son to become genuinely human. (Just think of all those disgusting bodily functions!) And so they argued that Christ only "appeared" to be human, but never actually was. They are called Docetists, from the Greek word meaning "seem"; we might call them the Seemists.

At the other end of the spectrum, some argued that Jesus was not fully divine. They are often called Arians, from Arius, whom tradition has identified as the originator of this idea.

Those at the center (what turned out to be mainstream Christianity) wished to emphasize that Jesus was both fully human and fully divine. Christmas reminded believers of his fully human nature—being genuinely born human to a human woman is surely the ultimate test of humanity. The rituals and celebrations associated with Christmas emphasized that fact.

And the Epiphany should remind believers that Jesus was fully divine, too. The Greek word means "manifestation" or "appearance," and so indicates the day on which Jesus' divinity was manifested or revealed to humankind.

But what event in Christ's life would best serve as the marker of the revelation of his divinity? Opinions differed.

Some maintained that Christ's birth itself was the moment of manifestation. Others argued for his baptism. The visit of the magi seemed to make sense, too. Wasn't that the moment at which Jesus' divinity was revealed to the outside world? Others thought Jesus' first miracle, at the marriage at Cana, was the first incident to reveal his divinity.

In western Christianity, the magi ultimately won out. And so the Epiphany is the celebration of the manifestation of Christ when the magi visited Bethlehem.

29. What were the Saturnalia, and what do they have to do with Christmas?

The Saturnalia were the days of the Roman winter solstice festival.

It seems likely that Saturn was originally an agricultural deity and that the Saturnalia started off as festivities to celebrate the last sowing before the onslaught of winter. The festival would begin with a splendid sacrifice to Saturn, followed by a large, informal, probably rowdy banquet. After the banquet, people would head off to celebrate with their friends and families.

The streets of Rome were full of people making merry and gambling, something that was not permitted in public at other times. Even slaves and children took part in these activities. In fact, a temporary "liberation" of slaves seems to have been one of the most distinctive features of the holiday. (Even the god was freed—the cult statue of Saturn, normally bound by woolen straps, was untied for the Saturnalia.)

Some masters and their families actually served the holiday feast to their slaves—an explicit role reversal, and so not unlike later Christmas holiday role reversals. In other households, the slaves would eat a lavish feast in the family's dining room, where they would normally be serving, not eating, while the master and his family waited their turn in another room. Everywhere wine was flowing. At many a house, a Saturnalian "king" would be selected by lot, and even slaves might play this part. The "king" would be a sort of master of ceremonies and master of mischief, with the authority to compel other revelers to do ridiculous things for everyone's amusement.

Technically, the day of the Saturnalia was December 17, but like Christmas, the Saturnalia were really a "season." The festivities sometimes lasted a full seven days.

In deciding to celebrate Christmas on December 25, the Church decided to compete with the worship of the most prominent pagan deity of the late Roman Empire, the Unconquered Sun (Sol Invictus, or Mithras). But Christianity was simultaneously competing with the Saturnalian festivities, the most beloved festivities among the Romans and the ones they were most reluctant to abandon. And so the Church essentially co-opted the Roman celebration and Christianized it. But the Saturnalia, one might say, also paganized the Church. The celebration was now in honor of Christ, but some of the traditional pagan activities continued.

Here's an example: We would expect any predecessor of our Christmas celebration to include the exchange of presents, and gift-giving was in fact an important part of the Saturnalia. In ancient sources, we even hear very familiar complaints about the whole process. The Roman poet Martial, for example, sulks about giving but not receiving gifts and makes it perfectly clear that the Romans were very conscious of how much their friends and relatives spent on them. Here's a loose translation:

> For the Saturnalian holiday:
> When he was poor, Umber'd give me a mink,
> Now that he's rich, he just spots me a drink!

Martial even accuses an acquaintance, perhaps in jest, of giving him an unappetizing sausage that the acquaintance had received as a Saturnalia gift from someone else!

Martial also gives us a pretty good idea of the sorts of things Romans received as Saturnalia gifts. The list is amusingly familiar and yet quite bizarre: whips, rods, parasols, clothes, pigs, dice, wine, hair (for wigs), a discus, crystal, axes, a flyswatter made of peacock feathers, olives, toothpicks, sponges, bowls, tables, money, parrots, slaves, books, jars of figs, a ball made from a bladder, and even a cook.

You can experience a bit of the ancient Saturnalia in Rome today, although you'll need to use your imagination. Start off at the Christmas market in the Piazza Navona; ancient Rome, too, had its own winter festival market (though elsewhere in the city) where people shopped for Saturnalia gifts. Next, head to the Forum, where you can see the impressive remains of the temple of Saturn near the base of the Capitoline hill. That's where the grand Saturnalian sacrifice took place. Then, walk down to the Colosseum, as the ancient Romans would have done, where one year the emperor hosted the public banquet; gourmet foods rained down from ropes suspended across the width of the Colosseum to the banqueteers below. Finally, if you have time, head to Ostia, just a bit outside Rome (and a fascinating place in any event), whose remains of ancient apartment houses and homes can transport you to the world of domestic Saturnalia celebrations. You can even picnic there.

30. What does Yule mean?

*Y*ule is a very old Scandinavian word for Christmas. (To this day, "God Jul," pronounced "gudt yool," means "Good Christmas" in Swedish.) But why and in what context does this word appear in English in the Christmas season?

From the ninth to the eleventh centuries, Danes controlled much of England. Along with their weapons, they brought their own term for Christmas, *Yule*, which eventually became an English synonym for Christmas. In similar fashion, *Yuletide* came to mean "the Christmas season."

Most authors argue that the Vikings and other medieval Scandinavians had an ancient pagan winter festival called Yule. According to this view, Christianity co-opted both the Yule festival and the word itself, but shifted the focus of the celebration to Jesus' birth and attempted to moderate some of its wilder elements. Other writers maintain that the Christmastide festival was essentially new to the Scandinavians, and so the name "Yule" does not reflect any earlier pagan rites. (Appropriately, the word Yule may be a distant cousin of the English word "jolly"!) Unfortunately, the Vikings and their kin were not concerned about what we would make of their festivities and did not leave us enough pre-Christian evidence to know for certain what "Yule" meant to them before their Christianization.

The Yule log, then, is a Christmas log, but of a very peculiar kind. As early as the seventeenth century in Europe, young men from many households would head into the forest to fetch a special Christmas, or Yule, log. They went in groups because the log would be enormous—no single man could drag it back, and occasionally horses were required to do the job. Some households would acquire the log well in advance of Christmas in order to let it dry out. Other households would fetch the log on Christmas Eve, and this quest would be an important part of the Christmas festivities. The log would be kindled and expected to burn for the entire day, sometimes for more than a day.

The household would not allow the log to be completely consumed, however. A fragment would be saved and carefully preserved for the next Christmas, when it would be used to kindle next year's Yule log. This practice suggests that the Yule log was considered to have magical properties, a suggestion that other evidence confirms. Some folks thought that the ashes from the log could protect the household from ghosts, and we even run into the idea that the ashes from the Yule log could cure toothaches! (This sort of "medical" thinking has parallels in the ancient world. Roman charioteers, for example, would drink cocktails of dried dung to help cure their bumps and bruises. The emperor Nero, a big chariot-racing fan, would drink this potion just to be identified with them!)

Those of us with twentieth- or twenty-first-century fireplaces might be amazed that a log huge enough to burn for an entire day and beyond could be fit into a fireplace. But early fireplaces were built so as to accommodate enormous logs, which were often the only means of heating the home and cooking its meals. When most homes in Europe and America began to use other modes of heating, fireplaces became smaller. Too small, sadly, for Yule logs. Coal, natural gas, and electricity thus contributed to the demise of the Yule log.

But the Yule log is not entirely extinct. Some British pubs have revived the Yule log tradition. Those of us with small fireplaces and correspondingly small logs nonetheless think of our Christmas blazes as Yule fires. And, surely most important, the French had the good sense and taste to transform the vanishing Yule log into a chocolate cake, the "Buche de Nöel" ("Christmas Log"), which appears in bakeries and confectionaries around Christmas. The most elegant of these logs are so carefully crafted to resemble real logs that they even have marzipan mushrooms on their bark. Thankfully, many other nations that have abandoned the original Yule log have adopted the edible version. Check the bakeries in your town.

31. What's a wassail?

*I*t's a toast. It's a drink. It's a bowl. It's a ritual. It's a form of begging.

The whole thing got started in the Middle Ages, when it became customary for someone, presumably the host of the gathering, to utter the toast "Waes hail"—that is, "To your health"—while handing someone else a bowl of potent brew. The recipient would respond, "Drinc hail"—that is, "A drink to *your* health"—and take a drink. This little ritual would be repeated again and again as the bowl circulated around the gathering. This toast, "Waes hail," evolved into our word "Wassail," which came to stand for the entire ritual.

Over time households designated a special bowl for this ritual, which was called, naturally, the wassail bowl.

It is easy to imagine how this festive custom contributed to the participants' feelings of intimacy and connection, especially since the wassail was passed in the Christmas season. It is reminiscent in some ways of ancient ritual oath-taking, by which the authority of the gods bound pagans to one another for different purposes.

But at some point, probably in the late sixteenth or early seventeenth centuries, a new form of wassailing was added to that just described. Poor folks, not infrequently women, would go around to the households of the wealthy. Bearing a filled wassail bowl, they would sing carols and beg for hospitality and a gift, often food or money, in return for a taste from their wassail bowls.

What sort of drink were poor wassailers offering? Recipes changed from place to place and from time to time, but most of them sound pretty unappetizing to our ears. You might be drinking a concoction of ale, eggs, spices, and cream. Roasted apples and even toast might be swimming in the brew.

Today, we tend to associate wassailing with caroling, a historically legitimate association considering that song was an essential part of the wassailing of the poor long ago. The most popular version of the "Wassail Song" (aka, "Here We Come A-Wassailing"), for example, is really about caroling. But with the modern tendency to romanticize Christmas customs of the past, we have forgotten that most early peripatetic wassailers went about singing and begging in the cold of winter because they lived in oppressive poverty. And this fact is reflected in the lyrics of many a wassailing song.

> We are not daily beggars
> That beg from door to door,
> But we are neighbours' children
> Whom you have seen before . . .
>
> Good Master and good Mistress,
> While you're sitting by the fire,
> Pray think of us poor children
> Who are wandering in the mire . . .

Yes, poor children took part, but not out of love for caroling.

32. Had children "better watch out"?

_A_bsolutely, _if you were a naughty child living before the_ second half of the nineteenth century.

We tend to think of Christmas as an opportunity to give our children lots of gifts. In contrast, earlier generations saw an opportunity to issue children report cards on their character development. A poem of 1821 that appeared in _A New-Year's Present to the Little Ones from Five to Twelve_, for example, expresses this view rather menacingly:

> (Santa:)
> But where I found the children naughty,
> In manners rude, in tempers haughty,
> Thankless to parents, liars, swearers,
> Boxers, or cheats, or base tale-bearers,
>
> I left a long, black, birchen rod,
> Such as the dread command of God
> Directs a parent's hand to use
> When virtue's path his sons refuse.

Yipes! Santa not only leaves the rod for the parents to use on the naughty child, but adds God's weight to the recommendation for a beating.

Two factors seem to have made these annual "evaluations" particularly effective. First, the evaluation consisted not of something abstract like a number, letter, or symbol, but of real, palpable rewards and punishments. Second, although Santa's assessments verified what parents had been telling their children ad nauseum throughout the year, they did not appear to emanate from the parents. They were an independent verification of parental assessment. In effect, Santa proved that Mom and Dad must be right.

Children who failed their Christmas evaluation would generally receive nothing or something unappealing in their stockings. To make the moral point all the more effectively, though, some parents would put a rod or switches in their children's stockings. And in an effort to make the whole event even more painful and humiliating, these parents did not hesitate to lavish gifts on some of their children while giving nothing but a rod to others. (Some surviving accounts of these tragic holidays suggest that the favored siblings tended not to be terribly sympathetic to the punished.)

In many places in Europe, and also in nineteenth century Pennsylvania, Santa employed an aide who would do the evaluating and not infrequently give the naughty children their "presents." The ritual varied from place to place, but the routine would typically proceed as follows.

Around St. Nicholas' Feast Day, when "Christmas" presents were usually (and in some places still are) given to children, Santa's agent—very likely a villager in disguise—would show up at the door. The agent would then quiz the parents about the children's behavior in their presence. If the parents' report was negative, the agent would give them a rod and, like the poem quoted above, recommend that the parents make good use of it. (Samuel Taylor Coleridge, the British Romantic poet, has left us a fine account of this practice in his "Christmas at Ratzeburg.")

I'm glad to report that by the end of the nineteenth century, as Christmas was more and more dedicated to pleasing children, for the most part Santa had given up his role in disciplining them.

33. Has Christmas ever been suppressed in a Christian country?

*Y*es. *For a while in the seventeenth century, Puritans* in Massachusetts and England outlawed the celebration of Christmas.

One of the goals of the radical Puritans in both Great Britain and America was to eliminate all forms of Christian cult and celebration that could not be found in the Bible. They considered non-biblical practices either remnants of paganism or inventions of loathed Roman Catholicism. Either of these associations, they believed, were offensive to God and needed to be "purified" right out of Christianity.

Although the Puritans did not deny that Jesus had been born, they pointed out that the Nativity accounts in Matthew and Luke said nothing about the date of Christ's birth. If God had wished Jesus' birth to be celebrated, they argued, God most certainly would have made the date explicit in the New Testament. Christmas festivities, they also noted, were adaptations of pagan festivities. And the Puritans were particularly appalled by the wildness of much of the traditional celebration of the holiday. The influential Puritan preacher Increase Mather perfectly expressed the confluence of the Puritans' theological and moral reservations: "The Feast of Christ's nativity is attended with such profaneness, as that it deserves the name of Saturn's Mass, or of Bacchus his Mass, or if you will, the Devil's Mass, rather than to have the holy name of Christ put upon it."

And so, between 1659 and 1681 it was illegal to celebrate Christmas in the colony of Massachusetts.

Although the New England Puritans were not able to eradicate utterly the celebration of Christmas, they did succeed in significantly reducing popular participation and even consciousness of the holiday. Historical records for that period rarely mention Christmas festivities or their suppression—the law seems to have been effective for the most part—and even the very mention of Christmas disappears from most New England almanacs, as though it no longer existed.

Throughout much of the 1640s and 1650s, Britain's Puritan Parliament tried to suppress the celebration of Christmas in England as well. They were determined to reduce December 25 to the status of any ordinary day. Business as usual. And so Parliament pointedly met on Christmas Day. They tried to keep shops open and churches closed. They were not very successful with the shops. Most businesses closed, and when shopkeepers and the authorities tried to keep them open, armed apprentices and their allies would sometimes fight to preserve their cherished day off. And despite these government efforts, a great many people continued to celebrate the holiday in the privacy of their homes. Popular attachment to the secular festivities and revelry proved impossible to eradicate.

Ironically, the Puritans were actually more successful in suppressing the *religious* celebration. The English countryside proved difficult to police, but in towns and cities the authorities were able to prevent parishioners from decorating their churches with winter greenery and from attending services.

With the restoration of the British monarchy, Puritan rule ended—and so did official suppression of the holiday. The public celebration of Christmas made a comeback.

34. Has children's anticipation of Christmas ever fomented rebellion?

$\mathcal{C}$hildren may be heartened to hear that Christmas has indeed played this subversive role!

Starting in the sixteenth century, it was not uncommon for British boys to occupy and barricade their schools, but not against some foreign enemy. The custom was called "barring out," since its immediate goal was to bar the schoolmaster from the school. The boys' ultimate goal, however, was to win concessions from him. The sources suggest that barring out, although it occasionally occurred at other times of the year, was particularly associated with the Christmas season.

British education before the twentieth century was very different from our own. The emphasis was not on inspiring the child's imagination and fostering intellectual flexibility and curiosity—or even on imparting critical thinking skills. Rather, as Sir John Eardley Wilmot put it in the eighteenth century, "To break the natural ferocity of human nature, to subdue the passions and to impress the principles of religion and morality, and give habits of obedience and subordination to paternal as well as political authority, is the first object to be attended to by all schoolmasters who know their duty."

To effect this discipline, the schoolmaster was a law unto himself. And he enforced his law by beating his students with a rod. Many schools even included an image of a rod on the school seal! More than one schoolmaster was notorious for his cruelty, and it was not unheard of for the aggrieved parents of children who had received a particularly severe flogging to attack the schoolmaster.

The students exacted their own revenge, as well. As the Christmas season neared, some schoolboys would plan and prepare to take their school, which not infrequently consisted of a single room. On a day kept secret from the schoolmaster, the boys would seize the school and declare their unwillingness to relinquish control until their demands were met. The demands often consisted, not surprisingly, of relief from their steady diet of beatings and an extension of their Christmas holiday.

Some of these rebellions approached the ferocity of a military campaign. According to an eyewitness, in 1789 the boys of the Royal School, Armagh, Ireland, assembled money, food (especially cheese), and weapons. Toward midnight, they occupied the dormitory and commenced destroying the staircase that led up to it. When the schoolmaster arrived to stop the destruction of the stairs, the students fired their pistols (the author claims that they were not actually firing at the schoolmaster!), and the staircase came crashing down as the master retreated. In the morning, some of the boys were lowered from the dormitory by rope and robbed the local baker's deliverymen at gunpoint. That morning the students also sent down their terms, which consisted, apparently, of a demand for more vacation days. Some soldiers were brought up to address this insurrection, but when the boys fired on them, they withdrew. After another day of siege, though, the rebels surrendered. When a bullet "fired across the court entered the Master's wife's bedchamber passing within an inch of her head," the good lady wrote the mutineers a letter that induced them to capitulate. Teachers everywhere will be dismayed to hear that the miscreants were not punished, for they had made amnesty one of the conditions of their surrender.

Extraordinary examples aside, in many instances these Christmas schoolboy rebellions were a kind of ritual, with customs and conventions and, occasionally, even written rules. In some places, refreshments accompanied the barring out, and townspeople and officials would show up to see the event while enjoying a snack and a drink.

Why was Christmas the season of insurrection? As I've already suggested, students often demanded an extension of their Christmas break. In those days the schoolmaster determined the length of the holiday, and so the boys would need only his consent to escape school for an extra day or two. It is not difficult to imagine—especially for parents of young boys—how attractive this rowdiness and inversion of the normal scholastic hierarchy must have been for the students. This attraction probably intensified as their temporary liberation—that is, Christmas vacation—approached. Any teacher knows that students become more restless as holidays draw near.

But the real question is, why did the authorities put up with this open insurrection right before Christmas? The Christmas season had been a time of release and license for centuries, probably as far back as ancient pagan mid-winter celebrations. Those in power had long realized, if not always on a conscious level, that to maintain their position they would need to allow people occasional opportunities to violate the normal rules of society and blow off steam, for the vast majority of the common folk had bleak prospects and very difficult lives. And what better time to let them vent than at the darkest, coldest, most inactive time of the year, especially since tradition had ordained this a time of excess? Many schoolmasters clearly felt the same way.

Incidentally, British colonists brought barring out to North America as well. For colonial and early American schoolboys, barring out was one of the most beloved elements of the Christmas season.

35. Is Christmas commercialism new?

*N*o, *aggressive marketing and lavish spending have long* been a Christmas tradition.

As early as the eighteenth century, advertisements for holiday presents appeared in European magazines, but the explosion of Christmas commercialism took place in the nineteenth century. At the time, some people found the growth of holiday materialism disturbing. In 1897, England's preeminent playwright, George Bernard Shaw, felt that "Christmas is forced upon a reluctant and disgusted nation by the shopkeepers and the press; on its own merits it would wither and shrivel in the fiery breath of universal hatred." A few years earlier, the *New York Tribune* had decried the torture of Christmas shopping in an article titled, "The Seamy Side of Christmas."

Gift-giving was not new, however. Winter solstice gifts go back at least as far as the Romans. Later, Europeans of means gave holiday presents to their dependents, servants, and tradespeople. Their gifts were in some ways closer to gratuities and would often consist of food, drink, money, and hospitality. Butchers and wine merchants probably rejoiced as the Christmas season drew near, but there was really little manufacturing or marketing directly related to Christmas and so no industries working overtime to stock the shelves.

With the industrialization of much of the western world in the nineteenth century, however, came the means to mass-produce items we today recognize as holiday gifts—toys, clothes, and the like. More important, though, industrialization produced a prosperous and ambitious middle class that was happy to see the more traditional boisterous Christmas mayhem replaced by quiet, controlled domestic celebrations. As a result, giving became a family activity, and family members—especially children—replaced clients as the principal recipients of Christmas largesse.

Of course, new kinds of presents were needed for this new kind of Christmas. Manufactured goods (at first, especially books and toys) replaced the traditional lump of mutton, which really would not do for the six-year-old.

Business folks became more aggressive in trying to satisfy (and excite) the need for manufactured presents. The advertising of holiday gifts gobbled up countless pages in newspapers and magazines. Promotional gimmicks abounded. Store window displays became increasingly spectacular; in 1883, Macy's presented steam-driven moving figures. In Philadelphia, confectioners baked colossal cakes and made candies shaped like lobsters and cockroaches. One British seller offered purchasers of his Christmas diaries an insurance policy against death in a train wreck.

Retailers took drastic steps that seem to us today all too familiar, in some cases for their lack of holiday spirit. In 1867, Macy's did not close its doors on Christmas Eve until midnight. The magnate F. W. Woolworth considered Christmas the perfect time to unload otherwise unsaleable products on a desperate and gullible public and warned his store managers to be particularly vigilant in the Christmas season for theft both by customers and employees.

We may wax nostalgic today about the good old noncommercial Christmas days that none of us has ever known, but Jo in Louisa May Alcott's *Little Women* knew better: "Christmas won't be Christmas without any presents."

36. Is Christmas dangerous to your health?

*I*t depends on who you are and what you do.

As recently as twenty years or so ago, it was assumed that epidemics of depression and suicide accompany all that Christmas cheer. In the *Spectator* in 1962, for example, one writer even claimed that "coroners, like most other professions, experience a Christmas rush"! Newspapers, television, and popular magazines, especially those catering to women, served up a steady diet of articles that promised to help us survive the Christmas blues. Some magazines and television programs still do.

The only problem with this assumption is that it is most probably incorrect.

No doubt about it: The Christmas season can be stressful, and some people become particularly depressed—the holiday blues syndrome even has a name and an apt acronym, "Seasonal Affective Disorder," or SAD. That holiday depression can even help drive the most seriously affected to take their lives. But SAD is actually related to the deprivation of light that winter brings, and recent studies seem to indicate that suicide rates go down at Christmas. According to one study, in fact, December has the lowest suicide rate of any month.

People who view Christmas principally as the commemoration of Christ's Nativity should be particularly encouraged. Study after study has suggested that religion can help preserve health and extend life. This is especially the case when the believer worships with a congregation. Human interaction is intrinsically healthy, and communities of believers tend to lend support when one of their own is ill. That Christmas Eve service does a body good!

Many religious people are also moderate in their habits, and this helps too. Recent scientific studies suggest that the moderate consumption of alcohol can actually be good for you. It is equally well established that the excessive consumption of alcohol is not.

And so to return to the question, it depends on who you are and what you do. If you are a person of faith, an active member of a congregation, a moderate drinker and eater who enjoys the companionship of family and friends, *and* you know how to enjoy yourself—happiness and laughter are healthy—then Christmas is probably good for you.

But if you are a grouchy, hard-drinking, antisocial atheist, you may not fare so well. Perhaps Dickens' Christmas spirits were saving Scrooge's health as well as his soul.

37. How do savvy merchants convince us to spend so much at Christmas?

Their strategies are numerous. So we'd all better watch out! Christmas purchases account for approximately one-sixth of all retail spending in the United States. For most retailers, this is the difference between success and failure. Obviously stimulating our impulse to buy during the holiday season is big business—and so the techniques they use to spur this impulse have become increasingly sophisticated and subtle.

We all complain about the ever-earlier appearance of Christmas displays and decorations in shopping malls and neighborhood stores during the fall. These days Halloween jack-o-lanterns and skeletons are scarcely out of windows before the reindeer appear. Yet dancing Santas and forty-foot mall trees are only the most visible part of the Christmas marketing push. The cleverest department store managers and shop owners lure us in through all of our senses.

Scent can be one of the most powerful and subtle lures. As early as the Middle Ages, vendors in market stalls used herbs to freshen the air and attract customers to their wares. Today managers may waft the scent of cinnamon or cloves through their store ventilating systems, using these familiar and homey smells of Christmas to put customers in a relaxed and celebratory mood. During one Christmas season, British Woolworth stores sprayed mulled wine dissolved in carbon dioxide into the air every quarter hour! Such scent strategies may have a more potent impact than we realize. The "smelling" part of the brain, the olfactory center, lies very near the part of our brain that is associated with emotions and cognitive behavior. Unsurprisingly, then, smells and emotions are often closely linked, and Christmasy scents that unconsciously call up memories of cozy, fireside festivities and celebrations with loved ones may actually make us more open-handed when we shop.

Retailers also know that the longer we spend in their shops, the more likely we are to buy something. Comfort is important. The right kind of sound also plays a role in keeping us happily browsing and shopping. Studies have shown that people spend up to 38 percent more time in stores where slow, calming music is played. Wise managers, then, play leisurely music over their sound systems—a harp and flute version of "Greensleeves," say, rather than a brass band rendering of "Jingle Bells." The few retailers kind (and smart) enough to give up floor space to customer seating also find their efforts to prolong our stay rewarded. Tired, uncomfortable shoppers buy far less than shoppers who have been reinvigorated by a short rest. Christmas displays placed within view of customer seating often sell briskly, too.

Color also influences people's buying habits. Fortunately for merchandisers at Christmas, red is a color that attracts customers, and savvy merchants exploit the holiday tie-in for all it's worth. Red is more arousing and stimulating to eye and brain than cooler colors such as green and blue, and so red is thought to be an excellent color for items customers might buy quickly, on impulse. Beware! Those red sweaters, socks, and stocking caps in the center aisle may have an attraction out of proportion to their intrinsic value.

Despite the rising percentage of e-commerce sales, many of us still like to take a "hands-on," more personal approach to holiday purchases. Offer us cups of hot spiced cider, and we'll stay to sip—and maybe buy the mix. Give us a slice of fruitcake and the next thing we know, we're ordering cakes for all our far-flung relatives. Retailers understand that humans are sensual beings, creatures of taste and touch, and so they offer us things to eat and place cashmere sweaters on waist-level displays right inside the entry to the store, where we can stroke and fondle them before deciding to buy. And of course you've noticed that the cuddly teddy bears that blink and say hello get prime toddler space in the shelves a foot-and-a-half from the floor.

So when we go Christmas shopping, we must always keep in mind that we are engaging in a battle of wits. And the competition is formidable—an entire field of study combining social science and marketing has developed to investigate who we are as consumers and how we shop. To keep the playing field level, *we* need to know who *they* are and how they sell.

38. What are the
Twelve Days of Christmas?

The twelve days from Christmas Day, on December 25, to the Feast of the Epiphany, on January 6.

Another legitimate answer, though, is that the twelve days *are* Christmas.

In earlier times, and especially in the Middle Ages, Christmas was thought of not as a day, but as a season, one that lasted the twelve days starting December 25. At many manors, field work was suspended for the entire twelve days, and many workers were permitted to be idle for most of the period.

Six of the days had particular liturgical and festive significance:

December 25:	Christmas Day
December 26:	St. Stephen's Day (honoring the first Christian martyr)
December 27:	St. John the Evangelist's Day
December 28:	Feast of the Holy Innocents (the children murdered by Herod)
January 1:	New Year's Day/Commemoration of Jesus' Circumcision
January 6:	Epiphany/Twelfth Night (the official end of the Christmas season)

These special days were also associated with special activities and traditions. New Year's Day, for example, became the principal day for giving gifts, although in many places it ultimately lost that role to Christmas Day. To celebrate the Feast of the Holy Innocents, in some places Boy Bishops ruled, and puzzling events, including strange whipping rituals, took place. (The reason for this brutality remains unclear: a reminder of Herod's atrocity? A pagan survival of a ritual intended to drive out evil spirits?) On the Epiphany, the Star of Bethlehem might be suspended from the church's ceiling, and a king might make offerings (even gold, frankincense, and myrrh) to express his identification with the "Three Kings." Wine would be blessed (and much of it drunk) on St. John's Day, and horses would be blessed on St. Stephen's Day.

But above all, the days were dedicated to revelry and idleness. In some places the houses of the gentry were supposed to stay open to locals for the whole twelve days, although not everyone was so generous. Great feasting and drinking went on for these twelve days, and many artistic performances, as well, for the season was also known for its musical and theatrical presentations.

It was also a season full of mischief, and intimidating bands of drunken and disguised men were known to confront neighbor or stranger under the darkness of night. This kind of revelry may not have pleased the powers that were, but it allowed the lower classes to blow off steam for a limited and clearly prescribed time. When the holidays were over, the social and political hierarchy was still in place.

A noteworthy difference between our Christmas and that of the distant past is the different notions of what constitutes the Christmas season. We tend to think of it as the weeks preceding Christmas. Christmas Day itself is the culmination, and for many, December 26 is a considerable letdown.

The weeks before Christmas were not without event for medieval people, but for them the Christmas season really started on Christmas Day. And most of them celebrated for about two weeks.

39. What's Victorian about a "Victorian Christmas"?

*B*efore we can answer this, we have to ask what "Victorian" means.

Victoria was Queen of England from 1837 to 1901, the better part of the nineteenth century. During her reign, the British Empire enjoyed its greatest expansion, and Great Britain was the most powerful nation in the world. England was also in the vanguard of the nineteenth-century social, economic, and political revolutions that gave birth to the modern world. The English started the century as a nation of farmers and ended it as a nation of factory workers and merchants. And to enjoy the fruits of these workers' labors, a new industrial and commercial middle class emerged, grew, and came to dominate British culture.

Anything associated with Victoria's reign and the British Empire in the nineteenth century can appropriately be called "Victorian," but today the term is popularly applied to the values and tastes of England's new middle class—values and tastes that Victoria, to a significant extent, shared. Since the American middle class of that time largely followed the lead of its counterparts in the old country, "Victorian" is often legitimately applied to them as well. Older American towns and cities, for example, have quite a few "Victorian" houses.

The "Victorian" nineteenth century also laid the foundations for the modern Christmas. It would take several pages just to outline all the elements of Christmas as we know it today in America and England that were either introduced or significantly expanded in the nineteenth century. The Christmas card, gift-giving, Christmas trees, Charles Dickens' *A Christmas Carol,* Santa Claus—even Christmas carols experienced a significant revival in the Victorian period, and several of our most beloved and seemingly ancient carols were composed or rearranged in the nineteenth century ("We Three Kings of Orient Are" and "It Came upon the Midnight Clear" are two examples).

Magazines, stores, and museum gift shops these days sell many repro-
ductions of artifacts from authentic Victorian Christmases. "Victorian"
cards, toys, and decorations, for example, burgeon around the holidays, and
customers often appreciate their beauty, elegance, and quaintness. The ultimate appeal for many of us, though, is nostalgia. Every December we are
assaulted by garish decorations, offensive commercialization, and Ronald
McDonald as Santa, and we want to escape. And so we do . . . to the past. We
try to recapture a purer, more elegant, less commercial Christmas. The Victorian Christmas.

When we flee to the Victorians, though, we are trying to recapture a
Christmas that in some respects never existed and in most respects existed
only for a very few. It was precisely the emerging commercial class—about
whose pedigree and taste old aristocrats were less than enthusiastic—who
created and promoted the Victorian Christmas. For them, Christmas was
also a celebration of who they had become and how much they had acquired.
Money flowed. If anything, the Victorians set us on the road to today's mate-
rialistic Christmas.

The vast majority of Victorians could afford few if any of the elegant
decorations and presents that filled the houses of the middle class. It is no
accident that Karl Marx was a Victorian. London, New York, and other
exploding industrial cities were full of impoverished people trying to survive in disgusting and inhuman conditions. Many of them, disillusioned
with their Victorian Christmas, *their* contemporary Christmas, may have
dreamed of a good old-fashioned medieval Christmas.

40. Why do we give gifts at Christmas?

ecause pagans did.
They didn't actually give them at Christmas, of course, but rather at some of *their* great winter festivals, especially at the Roman Saturnalia.

Early Church leaders argued among themselves about how to respond to the power of pagan culture, especially because so many converts would not give up the traditional amusements and holiday celebrations that their forefathers had enjoyed. So in the face of a popular pagan practice, the Church generally acted in one of two ways—either it fought to eradicate it, often a losing battle, or it tried to adapt and then adopt it.

It was hopeless, for example, to fight against the popular winter solstice gift-giving, especially since there was really no compelling reason to forbid the exchange of gifts other than its pagan context. Christmas provided a substitute context—sanitized the custom, one might say—and provided thoroughly Christian precedent and justification.

The magi's gifts of gold, frankincense, and myrrh provided a biblical precedent. Through giving gifts at Christmas, Christians emulated their act of worship—in a sense, reenacted it. Besides, giving gifts could be justified as an expression of Christian charity. And in fact it became the custom for the well-to-do to bestow gifts on the less prosperous.

It is pretty clear, though, that the gifts we exchange with our family and friends and the gifts that Santa brings our children have very little to do with the magi or Christian charity or the Nativity. Perhaps, then, another answer to this question of why we give gifts at Christmas is because we want or even need to.

Researchers and thinkers of many stripes have dedicated thousands of pages to explaining the psychology, economics, and sociology of gift-giving. The consensus seems to be that exchanging gifts is a critical way for societies to strengthen ties and define relationships. That was certainly the case for the ancient Romans when they exchanged gifts at the Saturnalia. We may think of our own exchanges of gifts as personal acts, and they are, but when we give and receive we also participate in one of the most essential social interactions of our culture.

41. Where does the custom of hanging a stocking come from?

This custom may have been inspired by the story of St. Nicholas giving dowries to a poor man's three daughters. But in the end, this is one of many Christmas customs about whose origin we simply have no hard evidence. And so, as is often the case, we are reduced to speculation. We are not utterly without clues, however.

In French convent schools, the girls would hang their stockings at Christmas in hopes that the abbess would fill them with gifts. The abbess, in her triple role as patron of children, protector of the girls' virtue, and bestower of presents, seemed to play a role like that of St. Nicholas.

The fact that stockings are hung by the *chimney* also seems to suggest that St. Nicholas' benefaction inspired the custom. One late version of the story of St. Nicholas' kindness has him tossing the third bag of gold down the chimney. It would not have been unnatural for the girls in that story to have hung their socks by the chimney to dry after washing them. And in the miraculous world of St. Nicholas, it would not have been out of the question for his third bag of gold to have landed in one of the girls' stockings. Quite a shot, true, but nothing exceptional for the remarkable Bishop of Myra.

The very anonymity of this way of receiving a gift—you go to bed full of hopes and wake up the next day to receive gifts left behind by someone you have not seen—reminds us of St. Nicholas as well.

The evidence is circumstantial, certainly not enough to decide the case. But it seems that we may have to hold St. Nick responsible for all those nail and thumbtack holes in our mantles.

42. Why, long ago, were children allowed to be "Bishop for a Day" in the Christmas season?

In the Middle Ages, it was felt that the Christmas season was the perfect time for a ritualized—and temporary—reversal of the normal power structure. The Nativity, after all, represents the ultimate role reversal: Almighty God becomes the most helpless of all creatures, a human baby. For the Church, replacing powerful bishops with mere children reflected this reversal.

Two specific days of the Christmas season were considered to be particularly significant for children: the Feast of Saint Nicholas, on December 6, and the Feast of the Holy Innocents, on December 28. Saint Nicholas was the forerunner of Santa Claus and by the Middle Ages was the patron saint of children. The Holy Innocents were the children of Bethlehem whom Herod slaughtered, according to Matthew's Gospel.

In a great many dioceses throughout medieval Europe, a choirboy would be selected to play the role of bishop on either Saint Nicholas' day or on the eve of Holy Innocents' day. In garb duplicating what real bishops wore, these boys would preside over religious ceremonies. Typically, they would lead processions, preach, and go on one-day tours during which they would bless people and raise money—much of which they got to keep. At Toledo in Spain, all the technical skills of the Spanish theater were employed to endow the temporary office with splendor and wonder. "Angels" flew down from the ceiling of the cathedral to hand the Boy Bishop the accoutrements of his office. And at York Cathedral in England, a Protestant source charged, the Catholic Boy Bishop even officiated at the mass! In 1541, under Henry VIII, a proclamation suppressed the custom, describing Boy Bishops as follows: "children strangely decked and appareled to counterfeit priests, bishops, and women, and so be led with songs and dances from house to house, blessing the people and gathering of money." This procession often culminated in a party. At Padua in Italy, the Boy Bishop would end at the real bishop's palace. After some irreverent banter between the real and the boy bishops, the boy would ask for wine and social drinking would ensue.

The custom of the Boy Bishop had its logic, though. Then, as now, the Christmas season was full of good cheer and merriment. It is easy to imagine that many adults, both clerics and laypeople, found amusing the sight of a child parading around in the elaborate and extravagant vestments of a medieval bishop. The subversive suggestion of this reversal may well have provided a bit of satisfaction to the majority of medieval Christians who had no prospect of ascending to any position of authority. And the exchange provided everyone with an important religious reminder: We are all, finally, the same in the eyes of the Lord. Medieval and Renaissance visions of hell and the Last Judgment frequently depict bishops and nobles, splendidly attired in the robes of their stations, suffering indescribable torments. When better than the season surrounding the Nativity to remind believers of the paramount value of innocence?

Changing times doomed this once popular custom. Theaters started to squeeze out much folk and ecclesiastical entertainment. The revelry and apparent irreverence of the Boy Bishop did not fit the sobriety of the Protestant Reformation and the Catholic Counter-Reformation. By the mid-eighteenth century, the day of the Boy Bishop was over.

43. Who invented the Christmas card?

*T*he first Christmas card was the brainchild of Henry Cole, a remarkable Victorian Englishman.

Cole spent much of his life trying to marry industry to art. In the nineteenth century, England was in the forefront of the industrial revolution, but the revolution was controversial for a variety of reasons. Industrialization had caused jarring social dislocation and cruel poverty. Some critics considered factory work itself dehumanizing and degrading, and the ugliness of mass-produced goods contributed to the coarsening and defacement of British life. In a nutshell, some felt that by producing ugly products in an ugly way, the industrial economy was making an ugly society of ugly people. And so these thinkers and artists thought that England needed to return to pre-industrial production.

Henry Cole sympathized to a certain extent with those sentiments but knew it was impossible to turn back the clock and reject industrialization. Rather, he believed, his nation should see to it that its products were beautiful and functional whatever their means of production and no matter how trivial their use. A more beautiful society would result, but also a more positive bottom line. Cole expected elegantly designed British goods to conquer the international marketplace. And so he dedicated his public life to the reformation of design education and to the establishment of superior design standards.

The Christmas card was one of his earliest ventures and was fully in keeping with his ambition to bring quality design to everyday objects. To design the first card, in 1843 he commissioned John Calcott Horsley, an artist who ultimately became a Royal Academician and painted two frescoes for the Houses of Parliament. (These days, Horsley is best remembered for his opposition to the influence of French painting and in particular to the use of nude models—for this he was dubbed "Mr. J. C(lothes) Horsley"!)

Cole did not stop with cards but also manufactured toys and published quality children's books that were designed to, in his own words, "appeal to ... a little child's mind, its fancy, imagination, sympathies, affections." Today the companies and shops that at Christmas offer educational toys and books intended to stimulate our children's imagination are, really, doing business in the Henry Cole tradition.

Cole's others services and accomplishments are far too numerous to catalogue here, but the mention of a few should give an idea of the historical importance and creative versatility of the father of the Christmas card:

- With Prince Albert, Queen Victoria's husband, he organized and promoted the Great Exhibition of 1851.
- He was founding director of what became the Victoria & Albert Museum (again, working with Prince Albert).
- He established the first museum restaurant (at the V & A).
- He designed an award-winning tea set.

As for the first Christmas card . . . it is inscribed:

A Merry Christmas

And

A Happy New Year

To You

This first card has three illustrations: two narrow scenes of benefactors helping the poor flank a wider scene of a family enjoying its Christmas feast. The man and woman of the house and two of their daughters seem to be toasting the card's recipient.

The card itself was not without controversy, for in the family celebration a young woman is giving a little girl a drink from a wineglass; it's pretty clear that the little girl is drinking wine and is being abetted in this activity by one of her elders! Because of this, Cole and Horsley were criticized for promoting drunkenness.

44. Why is Christmas the most important holiday in our professedly secular country?

ecause we wanted it that way. But the process wasn't easy. If America had started out as a unified nation with universally shared traditions, values, and aspirations, it would have been much easier to settle upon holidays. But the thirteen colonies each had different laws and customs. Even the apparently inoffensive Thanksgiving holiday was slightly unpalatable to some. It was, in origin, a New England Puritan holiday, and some Americans were reluctant to observe a holiday whose roots lay in a religious creed with which they differed.

As for Christmas . . . how could a holiday that a significant section of the country (New England Puritans again) had tried to suppress become a shared, national holiday?

And so, well into the nineteenth century, the United States had very few official holidays, and those that existed were actually acknowledged by the individual states, not the nation.

Some Americans observed this situation with despair. How can we ever become a truly unified people, they asked, unless we share festivities that define and strengthen who we are and what we cherish as a nation? And so campaigns promoting Thanksgiving and Christmas as national festivals were waged. And they were effective. Between 1840 and 1861, a majority of the states that had not recognized Christmas as a holiday did so, and on June 26, 1870, Congress made Christmas a federal holiday.

A national hunger for holidays to celebrate certainly helped to bring this about. But there were other factors as well.

Whether state and federal governments were happy about it or not, in the nineteenth century Christmas had become America's most beloved holiday. Christmas celebrations antedated the birth of the United States and had the advantage of never having depended on government patronage. This helped to depoliticize the holiday, making it palatable to Americans of all political leanings. (Yankee Thanksgiving, by contrast, had acquired an abolitionist reputation in the slave south.)

Meanwhile, as America's middle class grew and focused its attentions increasingly on private and family life, Christmas moved with them out of the rowdy streets and into sedate parlors, emerging as the nation's principal family celebration. The press accelerated the process. We tend to think of the seasonal tidal wave of magazines focusing on Christmas as a recent phenomenon. But nineteenth-century magazines, too, boosted their circulation by dedicating considerable space to poems, stories, illustrations, and discussions of Christmas, enhancing readers' interest in and affection for the holiday.

A great historical event played a role as well: the Civil War. The war had divided millions of people from their loved ones. And at Christmas, in particular, the pain of the separation was most intense. For a nation torn apart, Christmas came to symbolize home, family, and peace, and the holiday emerged from the war years even more beloved than before.

Changes in the way America worked also helped make Christmas a national holiday. The rhythms of rural life had ensured that few folk dependent on the land needed to work on Christmas day. But in the nineteenth century, as the United States became more industrialized, factory owners, motivated by profit, were content to have their workers labor away on December 25. In response, new state and federal laws were enacted that made Christmas a legal holiday. Some of the evidence suggests that industrialists, too, supported this legislation, hoping that congressional action would *limit* the number of annual holidays to four.

But how were state legislatures and Congress able to recognize a *religious* holiday as a legal holiday without violating the Constitution's separation of church and state? It's not hard to understand. Though officially secular, the United States has been a quasi-Christian country for much of its history. Most nineteenth-century Americans were Christians of some sort. But at the same time, American Christmas was never a particularly Christian celebration anyway. For many, a combination of Old World pagan customs, such as Christmas greenery, and American secularizing adaptations, such as Santa Claus, had overwhelmed the religious observation. Commemoration of the Nativity was essentially a private event.

Technically, though, *Christmas* itself was not made a holiday, but rather the *twenty-fifth of December* was. The Congressional Act of 1870 declares: "An Act making the first Day of January, the twenty-fifth Day of December, the fourth Day of July, and Thanksgiving, Holidays, within the District of Columbia." Maybe Congress was really acknowledging the need for a very, very old-fashioned winter solstice celebration.

CHRISTMAS CHEER FOR THE UNFORTUNA

PEACE ON EARTH

45. How did Christmas become a time for charitable giving?

riginally through tipping, begging, and extortion.
Early Christmas charity took a variety of forms, most of them completely different from the donations to charitable organizations with which we today are most familiar.

By the late Middle Ages, in much of Europe the well-to-do were obliged in the Christmas season to open their doors to the less fortunate and to provide them with food and drink. The wealthy were not always scrupulous in doing their duty—some would even plan to be away at Christmas to avoid welcoming and subsidizing their social inferiors. Others would host only their immediate dependents, hardly the neediest folks in the district, and in some places tenants were obliged to bring food to the feast. *Poor Robin's Almanac* complained about aristocratic Christmas slackers in 1702:

> And fiddlers who used to get scraps
> Now cannot fill their hungry chaps;
> Yet some true English blood still lives,
> Who gifts to the poor at Christmas gives,
> And to their neighbours makes a feast,
> I wish their numbers were increased.

Over time various forms of begging developed, and the poor would make the rounds of the homes of the wealthy. Theirs was a highly ritualized form of begging, though, and usually entailed the fiction that an exchange was taking place. The poor would get food, drink, or even money; the rich would get some sort of entertainment.

Those in need might recite some verses, sing a song—one of the most common employments of the Christmas carol—perform a little drama, or even display something of supposed value and meaning, such as a decorated box containing dolls representing Mary and baby Jesus. In these instances, the charity was ostensibly a kind of tip for the performers. Poor people might also carry a wassail bowl to the homes of the wealthy in expectation of receiving something in exchange for a sip from their bowls. It was not unheard of, moreover, for roving bands of young men emboldened by alcohol and disguises to intimidate those from whom they solicited a contribution. *This* manner of seasonal begging bordered on extortion.

Tradespeople demanded their tips as well. By the seventeenth century, for example, English apprentices, servants, and others were receiving a Christmas cash bonus, sometimes placed in a fired clay box, which would be broken open to reveal the Christmas season's gratuities.

These customs were waning by the end of the nineteenth century as the philosophy and mode of Christmas charity shifted radically, and the modern style of charity was born.

As Europe and North America became more industrialized and urbanized, the established systems of giving based upon old-fashioned rural conditions and relationships served a shrinking percentage of the population, and not especially well. A gulf widened between the growing middle class, whose lives (and Christmases) centered more on their homes, and the mass of unemployed or poorly compensated urban workers crammed into slums. Private charitable organizations sprang up to bridge—and subtly to maintain—this gap. These organizations could spend contributions more efficiently than individuals could. They could also keep the scruffy poor at arm's length, since they eliminated the need for disagreeable personal contact with the needy. Besides, the thinking went, five dollars given directly into the hands of a poor man were likely to wind up in the hands of a barkeep. The extent of alcohol abuse in the nineteenth century suggests that this thinking was in fact all too often on the mark.

As the middle class grew more aware of the scale of the hardship and the desperation of the poor grew, magazines and newspapers focused regularly on the plight of the needy at Christmas. Their stories tended to focus on the "worthy" poor, especially children and women. Not coincidentally, many charitable organizations also focused on these two groups. The power of the press to evoke shame and pity and to set attitudes and inspire action saw to it that one priority of the season was the alleviation of the wretchedness of the unfortunate.

To this day, some charitable organizations intensify their fund-raising efforts at Christmas since, as Charles Dickens put it, "it is a time, of all others, when Want is keenly felt, and Abundance rejoices." When we donate, we participate in a form of charitable giving that began only in the nineteenth century.

46. When did Christmas cause an improbable truce in the midst of a savage war?

*I*n the year 1914.

By the end of 1914, fighting on the western front in World War I had caused about one million casualties. Those still alive were living in filthy, rat-infested trenches not unlike open graves. Neither side had made much progress in the fighting, and the future seemed to hold nothing but eternal misery and boredom occasionally punctuated by savage battle.

On Christmas Eve 1914, the sky cleared somewhat, and the air turned colder, crisper, fresher. The frost came as a relief to men who felt doomed to eternal rain and knee-deep mud. The change in the weather was a prelude to one of the most remarkable events in the war.

At one point on the front, lights appeared from the German trenches. Some British soldiers naturally assumed that an attack was imminent. To their astonishment, though, the Germans raised their voices, not their arms, and serenaded their British foes with "Stille Nacht" (that is, "Silent Night"). The lights, it turned out, were lights on small Christmas trees that the German infantrymen had erected and illuminated. Amazingly—and without authorization—infantrymen from both sides wandered out into no-man's land, the lethal wasteland between the two lines of trenches.

Variations on this scene were simultaneously occurring in many places along the lines. For the most part, the Germans initiated the truces. The enemies sang together, ate together, drank together. Soldiers even managed to come up with gifts to exchange. Some British infantrymen ate their Christmas dinner of 1914 in the trenches of their German enemies. At other spots along the line, German and British soldiers joined forces to bury their dead comrades whose neglected corpses had been decaying in no-man's land, some of them for weeks.

A spontaneous truce—or, rather, dozens of spontaneous truces—had occurred. Christmas, with its power to evoke home, tradition, brotherhood, and peace, had worked its magic.

Unfortunately, the soldiers' humanity only alarmed their leaders. (The Germans had actually supplied their infantrymen with the Christmas trees to intensify their love of their fatherland and so to inflame their desire to fight and die for it!) In some places, it was several days before the soldiers were willing to fight in earnest against an enemy with whom they had shared Christmas. But eventually everyone returned to the business of war. The German high command let it be known that they would consider future fraternization high treason. The British, too, made every effort to prevent the reoccurrence of spontaneous truces, and some officers threatened their men with the severest penalties. Christmas of 1915 saw very few such truces, and Christmas of 1916 saw none.

47. Have guns ever been part of Christmas celebration?

Y es, and quite often.

For many, Christmas is the commemoration and celebration of the birth of Christ, the prince of peace, and as such should be observed with dignity and contemplation. But throughout history, others have seen in Christmas an opportunity for mischief and mayhem, what scholars often call "misrule." The festive atmosphere of the season has been seen by many as an invitation to violate normal codes of behavior, to go wild. Such an atmosphere of "anything goes" existed in places in eighteenth- and nineteenth-century America, and gunfire frequently accompanied Christmas festivities.

We might expect merrymaking cowboys and trappers to be firing their weapons, but holiday gunfire was not limited to the Wild West. When officials in colonial New York, for example, outlawed shooting in the city on New Year's Eve, crafty New Yorkers seem to have moved the custom to Christmas, so that the state legislature eventually prohibited shooting on Christmas Eve as well. Government regulations were not sufficient, however, to extinguish the practice. It was not until the nineteenth century, when Christmas was transformed from a rowdy, public revelry into a sedate, family celebration, that merrymakers stopped shooting.

The firing of guns at Christmas was sometimes done according to very clear rituals. One such stylized practice, attested to in both the East and the West, was a kind of wassailing. Bands of men would make the rounds of their neighbors' houses and shoot off rounds in front of each home. The homeowners would then invite the armed revelers in for a (strong!) drink and a bite to eat. The band would then reload their rifles, drag the man of this most recent house along with them, and head on to the next house where the ritual would be repeated.

This is the aspect of Christmas shooting that may have made the practice particularly intimidating. Almost invariably, the shooters drank at each house, and it must not have taken too long for the shooting wassailers to feel the effects of their drinking. And yet it is hard to imagine a more potent combination than shooting and drinking for those who considered Christmas the occasion for a bacchanalian binge, as many did.

48. What do Hanukkah and Christmas have to do with each other?

*B*oth Christmas and Hanukkah are winter festivals. But beyond that obvious connection, there are other, more subtle connections as well.

First, though, what is Hanukkah? For most of the second century B.C., the Macedonian descendents of Alexander the Great's generals controlled the Middle East. In the 170s, one of these descendants, the powerful Antiochus IV, ruled over a vast Syrian empire that included Judea. Although he was a pagan, Antiochus even had the final say about who would be the Jewish High Priest of the Temple in Jerusalem. In 167 B.C., Antiochus inaugurated a campaign to compel the Jews to give up their ancestral way of life and their religion and to adopt Greek customs.

Antiochus forbade Jews to observe the Sabbath and to circumcise their sons, and he ordered the sacred Jewish texts, which Christians today read in the Old Testament, to be burned. The great Temple of Jerusalem, the center of Jewish worship of the God of Abraham, was now to be dedicated to the worship of the Greek god Zeus, and Antiochus pointedly instructed that the Temple be desecrated with the blood of pigs sacrificed to Zeus. These orders were more than a sacrilegious affront; they were tantamount to a declaration of war against Judaism. Without their sacred texts and law, and their traditional and distinctive form of worship and way of life, the Jews would be indistinguishable from pagans. And if they abandoned the God of Abraham for Zeus, they would be Jews in name only.

A country priest named Mattathias and his five sons (Judas Maccabaeus was the most prominent of them) spearheaded a rebellion and, despite being outmanned, retook the Temple. On the third anniversary of Antiochus' desecration, we are told, the Temple was rededicated to Jewish worship ("Hanukkah" means "dedication"). The relighting of the menorah, the Temple candelabra, was part of the rededication ceremony, but Antiochus' agents had been thorough in their defilement, and there was only enough pure burning oil for one day. Miraculously, however, the tiny supply of oil burned for eight days until a fresh supply of pure oil was procured.

Hanukkah, then, celebrates two miracles: the rebels' defeat of the much larger, professional forces of Antiochus and the miracle of the oil. Like the miracle of the Temple oil, the festival lasts eight days.

The recapture and cleansing of the Temple did not, however, bring an immediate end to the Jewish revolt and to Syrian dominance. For years after Judas Maccabaeus's victories, a Syrian garrison remained in Jerusalem, and Judea's leaders continued to be forced to acknowledge the power of Antiochus and his successors.

The Jewish rebels' greatest accomplishment, however, was not the semi-independence that they were able to gain for their people. The legions of the Roman Empire were on the horizon, and Jewish independence could be only of short duration. Rather, their triumph lay in the fact that their revolt thwarted Antiochus IV's attempt to eradicate the customs and identity of the Jewish people. Judas Maccabaeus and his followers, one could argue, saved Judaism.

Christian and non-Christian lovers of Christmas, then, are also indebted to the Jewish rebels. If Judaism had not survived as a belief, as a way of life, as a covenant with God, there would have been no Nativity, and so, no Christmas.

There is another connection as well. In the United States, at any rate, Hanukkah has become the most prominent religious festival for many Jews. This is due, to a significant extent, to the power of Christmas. Many Jewish writers have observed with concern that the Christmas season—with its decorations and festivities, not to mention its gift-giving—appeals to children of all faiths. How can Jews, some ask, preserve the identity and faith of their sons and daughters without robbing them of some of the fun and magic of Christmas celebrations? For many, the celebration of Hanukkah, done with care to stress its significance and traditions (that is, without allowing it to become "Jewish Christmas"), has been part of the answer.

49. Does Kwanzaa have anything to do with Christmas?

*K*wanzaa may seem to have nothing to do with Christmas other than being a winter solstice festival as well. It can, though, be viewed as both an alternative and a complement to Christmas.

Some think that Kwanzaa is an African religious festival. It is not, in fact, truly African or religious. A look at the origin of the festival may help clarify its nature.

In August 1965, six days of brutal racial violence occurred in the Watts section of Los Angeles. Thirty-four people died during those six days, and the property damage was estimated at $40 million. Watts was left in ruins, and the cultural and political future of African Americans seemed to some of them to be at a crossroads.

The riots and their aftermath suggested to black nationalist leader Maulana Karenga the need for African Americans to identify themselves and their culture as rooted in the very best of African culture and distinct from that of white America. Inspired by East African agricultural celebrations, in 1966 he created a festival that he named Kwanzaa, which means "first fruits" in Swahili.

Kwanzaa was meant to emphasize the African values that Karenga felt would be of the greatest use in promoting African American solidarity, independence, virtue, and prosperity: unity (*umoja*), self-determination (*kujichagulia*), collective work and responsibility (*ujima*), cooperative economics (*ujamaa*), purpose (*nia*), creativity (*kuumba*), and faith (*imani*).

So how is Kwanzaa an alternative to Christmas?

It was intended, in part, to offer an alternative to the commercial orgy of consumption that more and more marks the Christmas season in America. The activities of Kwanzaa—such as the lighting of the kinara (a candleholder with seven candles) in commemoration of African ancestors, the sharing of a simple meal, the discussion of the seven values of the holiday—are designed to emphasize education, thought, and community rather than acquisition.

How, then, can Kwanzaa be viewed as a complement to Christmas?

First of all, Kwanzaa is not denominationally affiliated. Christians can celebrate both holidays, and predominantly black churches in fact sometimes sponsor Kwanzaa-related events.

Second, Kwanzaa begins on December 26 and lasts seven days. This means that there is no scheduling conflict between Kwanzaa and Christmas.

But something else interesting is going on as well. The modern Christmas "season" has evolved over time away from celebrating the days following Christmas to celebrating the days leading up to it; Christmas spirit builds as December 25 approaches and deflates relatively soon afterwards. To a certain extent, the traditional Twelve Days of Christmas, from December 25 to January 6, have lost their function and meaning. For African American observers, Kwanzaa fills the vacuum. This festive "season" lasts seven instead of twelve days, but nonetheless resuscitates an age-old pattern of winter festivity.

50. Where can I learn more about Christmas?

*T*housands *of helpful books and articles have been written* about Christmas. I have relied upon the work of so many other writers that it is impossible for me to list all the texts that I have found informative and illuminating.

And so I offer you a handful of the books in English that have been among the most helpful to me in the preparation of this book. Some of them are scholarly, others are written for a more popular audience, but all are accessible. Not all of them are in print, unfortunately, but most are, and the ones that are not can still be found in some libraries.

Barnett, James H. *The American Christmas.* 1954. Reprint, North Stratford, N.H.: Ayer Company Publishers, 1984.

Baum, L. Frank. *The Life and Adventures of Santa Claus.* 1902. Reprint, New York: Gramercy Books, 1999.

Brown, Malcolm and Shirley Seaton. *Christmas Truce.* London: Leo Cooper/Secker & Warburg, 1984.

Brown, Raymond E. *The Birth of the Messiah.* Rev. Ed. Anchor, New York: Doubleday, Anchor Books, 1993.

Foster, Don. *Author Unknown. On the Trail of Anonymous.* New York: Henry Holt, 2000.

Golby, J. M. and A. W. Purdue. *The Making of the Modern Christmas.* Rev. Ed. Old Greenwich, Conn.: Sutton Publishing, 2000.

Guthridge, Ian. *All about Christmas.* Port Melbourne, Australia, 1988.

Highfield, Roger. *The Physics of Christmas.* Boston: Little, Brown & Co., 1998.

Hutton, Ronald. *The Stations of the Sun. A History of the Ritual Year in Britain.* Oxford: Oxford University Press, 1996.

Keyte, Hugh and Andrew Parrott. *The New Oxford Book of Carols.* Oxford: Oxford University Press, 1992.

Kidger, Mark. *The Star of Bethlehem. An Astronomer's View.* Princeton, N.J.: Princeton University Press, 1999.

Miles, Clement. *Christmas Customs and Traditions.* 1912. Reprint, New York: Dover Publications, 1976.

Miller, Daniel, ed. *Unwrapping Christmas.* Oxford: Oxford University Press, 1993.

Nissenbaum, Stephen. *The Battle for Christmas.* New York: Random House, Vintage Books, 1996.

Pimlott, J. A. R. *The Englishman's Holiday: A Social History.* Hassock, Eng.: Harvester Press, New York: International Publications Service, 1976.

Restad, Penne L. *Christmas in America: A History.* Oxford: Oxford University Press, 1995.

Scullard, H. H. *Festivals and Ceremonies of the Roman Republic.* Ithaca, N.Y.: Cornell University Press, 1981.

Snyder, Philip. *The Christmas Tree Book.* New York: Viking Press, 1976.

Trexler, Richard C. *The Journey of the Magi: Meanings in History of a Christian Story.* Princeton, N.J.: Princeton University Press, 1997.

Waits, William B. *The Modern Christmas in America: A Cultural History of Gift Giving.* New York: New York University Press, 1993.

Extremely useful, too, for finding information about books written before 1980 is Sue Samuelson's *Christmas. An Annotated Bibliography.* Vol. 4. Garland Folklore Bibliographies, 1982.

There are many fine collections of readings about Christmas. Two are particularly helpful to those of us trying to make sense of this most complex of holidays:

James, Francis G. and Miriam G. Hill, eds. *Joy to the World: Two Thousand Years of Christmas.* Portland, Oreg.: Four Courts Press, 2000.

Johnson, Pegram, III, and Edna Troiano, eds. *The Roads from Bethlehem. Christmas Literature from Writers Ancient to Modern.* Louisville, Ky.: Westminster/John Knox Press, 1993.